THE PICTORIAL GUIDE TO GROUP WORK ACTIVITIES

VOLUME TWO

GEOFF SANDERS

Acknowledgements

Thanks to all those people who have contributed ideas and offered assistance and encouragement in the creation of this book. With particular thanks to John West, Felicity West, Verity Carpenter and Bradley Carpenter.

Contents

INTRODUCTION

Since the publication of the first Pictorial Guide I have been collecting further ideas to put together for a second volume and, finally, hundreds of drawings later, and after much research, here it is. When I first considered the idea of producing a book about group work I wanted to record some of the best activities I had seen. At the same time I thought a book of this nature would be particularly suited to being presented in an entirely visual style using cartoon line drawings which have long been an interest of mine. The advantage of a pictorial book is that it eliminates the need for lengthy descriptive text and provides a format which is very easy to take in at a glance. Hence the reader is able to quickly scan the pages when looking for new ideas. The positive response to the first Pictorial Guide seemed to confirm this general theory.

The drawings are based on observations of groups working on activities and are designed to achieve visual clarity and an understanding of the purpose of each game.

The activities themselves are drawn from my own experience of group work and from the experience of other group workers from various professional backgrounds including Teaching, Youth Work, Social Work, Outdoor Education and Development Training.

Taken together volume 1 & 2 comprehensively covers a full range of activities from simple warm-up exersises through to the more challenging and complex ones illustrated in the sections on problem solving and organisation. These can be used to either supplement and enliven existing programmes or to create new ones.

Some further variations on well known themes have been included together with a number of original ideas which are appearing for the first time. UX III "Super Box" for example (page 93) was developed with this book in mind. They have all been tried and tested and can be further adjusted according to individual needs and circumstances.

SAFETY

All the activities should be properly supervised by responsible persons who can make an informed judgement about the suitability and the safety aspects that relate to any particular group.

The Author and Publishers cannot be held responsible in any way for any accidents or injuries that may occur during the course of these activities.

Once upon a time....

Warm Up

All the warm-up exercises require little preparation and only basic items of equipment, or non at all. They are easy to organise and lots of fun regardless of whether those participating know each other or not. Duck Pond (page 9) and Animal Farm (page 10) are particularly good for breaking down any initial inhibitions.

Activities on pages 16, 17 and 18 require whole team co-operation and effort and generate feelings of group achievement when the task is successfully accomplished.

True or false (page 23) and Clockwise (page 24) have been included in the section on communication but they are also good warm up games.

Duck Pond

① Divide the group into pairs at random. One person in each pair is selected to be the duck - the other to be the duckling. The participants are given two minutes to practice saying 'help' and ducks to say 'over here !' No other communication is allowed.

② Ducks and ducklings are now separated and all are blindfolded.

ducks

ducklings

③ On the command ducks and ducklings try to relocate their original partners.

over here

help

over here

help help

over here

help

over here

help

over here

help

Variation.   Each pair must invent its own location signal (no words allowed). If the members of the group are well known to each other, restrict the ducks to saying 'quack' and the ducklings to 'squeak'

Animal Farm

① Each person is given the name of a farm animal eg. Cow, Sheep, Pig, Dog etc.. Everyone is then blindfolded and scattered around a field/large area. There should be at least two people allocated to each animal type.

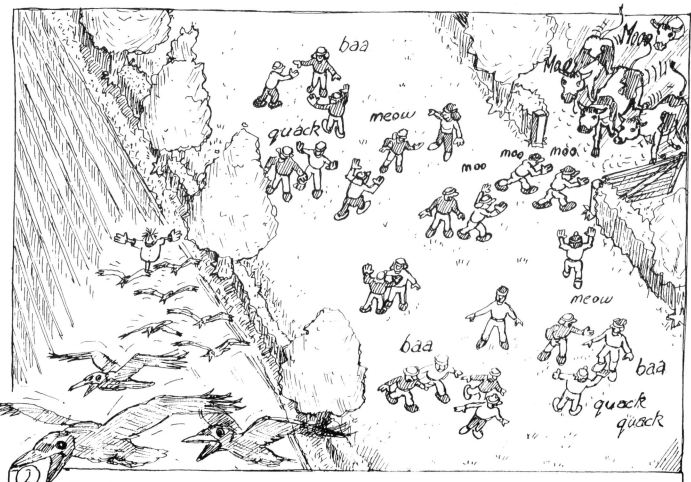

② On the command, everyone must locate their corresponding animals and form a herd, flock, pack etc. The only communication allowed is by making the characteristic animal sounds.

Channel Tunnel

①

② 1-2-3-lift!

How many times can someone pass through the tunnel before it collapses?

also see 'elevator' volume 1 (page 22)

Individuals are taken one at a time to a location which is out of sight of the rest of the group

① put on the blindfold and stand on the plank

② Rest your hands on Petes shoulders to steady yourself ....

③ Hold on !

④

⑤ OK, you're down !

⑥ previous participant

No Hands

Pin Ball Wizard

① In a circle facing outwards

one human "target" in the middle

missed!

② A soft ball is thrown in the manner illustrated at the target who tries to avoid being hit. If hit, the "target" swaps places with the thrower.

Roundabout

Hula hoops
or cycle tyres
(no letting go of hands)

The hoops must complete a circuit

Round Up

① Sitting in a circle, both hands holding on to a hoop of rope. no hands or elbows are allowed to touch the ground

No letting go of the rope

② On the command - stand up!

③

link hands
across

1-2-3 Stand

Stand Up

In pairs ...

Link arms

In a group

Chase the Chair

① A fast and hectic game providing lots of fun. Everyone takes a chair and puts them together in a tight circle. One person is selected to stand in the middle leaving one vacant seat. Everyone else sits down.

② The fun begins. Those sitting must move in a clockwise direction to occupy any vacant seat next to them. The person in the middle tries to find a vacant seat ...

change directions !

③ .. when they are successful the displaced person must try and find a seat and so on.

Communication

All groups and organisations need to communicate with individual members and with the wider world.

A communication system may be established simply to pass on messages and instructions from those in authority to those who carry out specific tasks.

Other systems may be part of a more complex process of consultation that encourages individuals to confront issues and to participate in the running of the group. In this way, personal and organisational development become interrelated

Any student who is about to take an examination should first take the 'Three Minute Test' on page 21. This demonstrates the importance of listening and checking information before taking action.

The other exercises cover the following areas:

Introductions	23, 24
Personal Images	25
Body Language	26
Co-operation	27
Individual Expression	28
Exclusive Groups	29
Values and Rules	30, 31
Descriptive Language	32, 33, 34
Directive Language	35, 36

Three Minute Test

Use this task to illustrate the importance of listening to instructions. Each person is presented with a list of 18 questions as follows ....

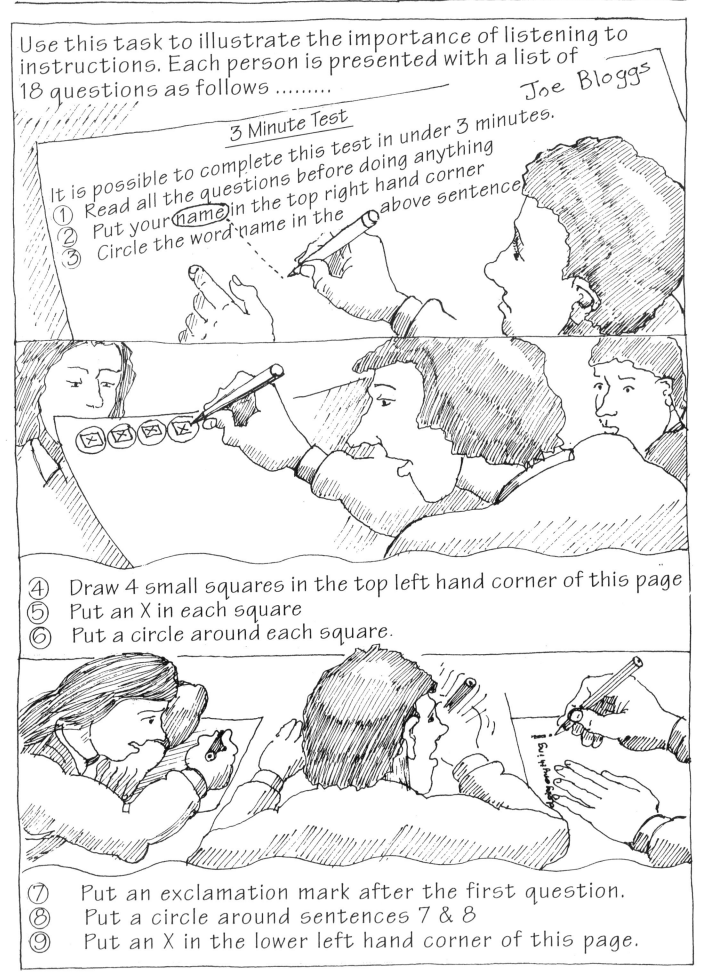

Joe Bloggs

3 Minute Test

It is possible to complete this test in under 3 minutes.
① Read all the questions before doing anything
② Put your (name) in the top right hand corner
③ Circle the word 'name' in the above sentence

④ Draw 4 small squares in the top left hand corner of this page
⑤ Put an X in each square
⑥ Put a circle around each square.

⑦ Put an exclamation mark after the first question.
⑧ Put a circle around sentences 7 & 8
⑨ Put an X in the lower left hand corner of this page.

Three Minute Test

True or False ?

① Each person in the group takes a sticky label. Tell everyone to write on their labels three statements about themselves. Two of the statements should be true and one should be false.

Each person displays their label

I support Manchester United FC

I am a good cook

I was born in Sheffield

② Direct everyone to turn to the nearest person (forming pairs) and to ask two questions about each of the statements

③ Q. What colour strip do Man Utd. wear ?
A. Red
Q. Which Man Utd. player was in the 1966 England Team ?
A. Er ...   (etc.)

④ You're not a Man Utd supporter
You're right !
O.K. your turn.

⑤

Move on to the next person around the whole group.

Clockwise

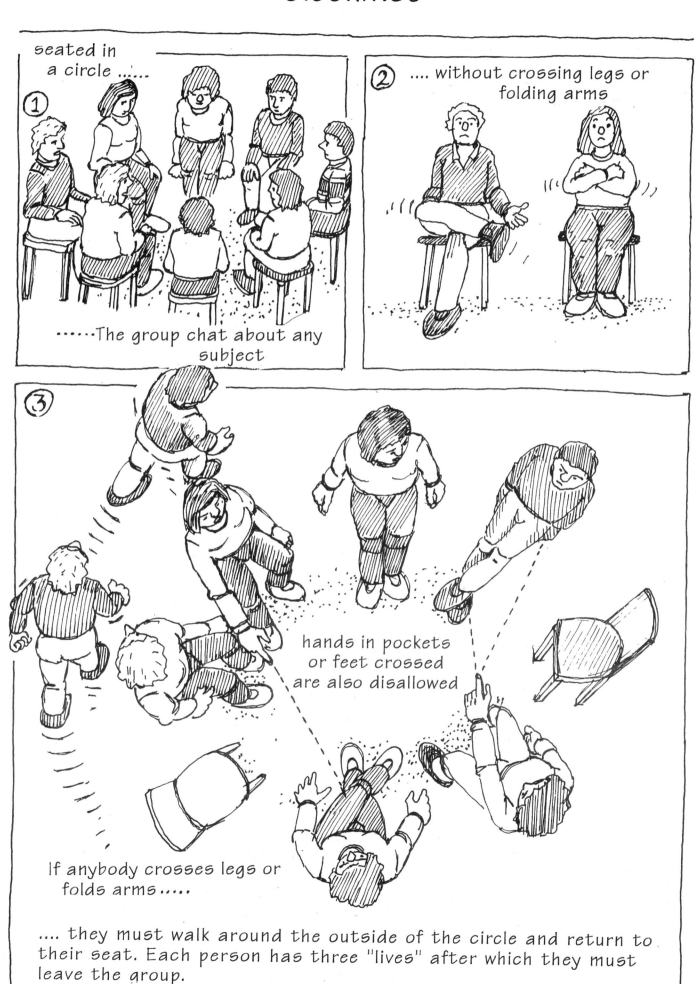

seated in a circle ......

① The group chat about any subject

② .... without crossing legs or folding arms

③ hands in pockets or feet crossed are also disallowed

If anybody crosses legs or folds arms.....

.... they must walk around the outside of the circle and return to their seat. Each person has three "lives" after which they must leave the group.

Guess Who

① John, concentrate on one other person in the group without making it obvious who it is.

② The rest of the group try to establish who John is concentrating on by asking questions in turn ....

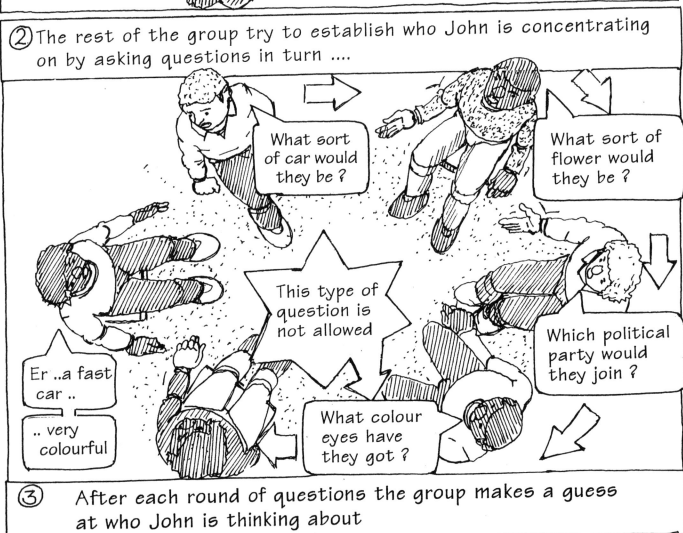

What sort of car would they be ?

What sort of flower would they be ?

This type of question is not allowed

Which political party would they join ?

Er ..a fast car ..

.. very colourful

What colour eyes have they got ?

③ After each round of questions the group makes a guess at who John is thinking about

Hand Jive

The Leader

1. In a circle, one person is selected to be the 'spotter' and they leave the room. A leader is now selected from those remaining. The leader directs the group in making various movements. The group practice following the leader.

2. The 'spotter' returns and tries to spot who is leading the group.

3. When the leader has been 'spotted' they become the next spotter and leave the room. A new leader is then selected and so on

4. Variation. 'Mirroring' in pairs

Where do you stand ?

①

Ten chairs are placed in a line

② Participants are presented with a number of statements eg. 'we should build more railways and fewer motorways'. Individuals are then asked to stand by whichever chair represents the strength of their feelings either for or against the statement.

strongly against

no strong feelings

Strongly in favour

③ The group is a strong team.

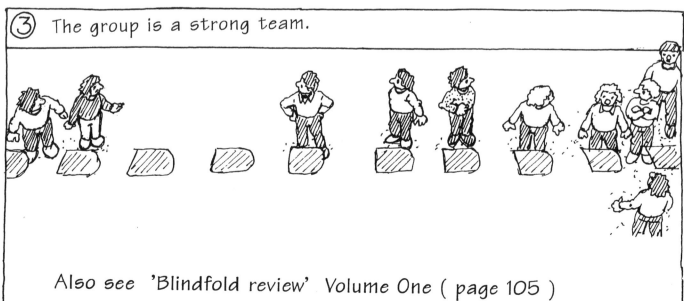

Also see 'Blindfold review' Volume One (page 105)

The Closed Group

①   In small groups. One person is selected to be the 'outsider' and leaves the room. Those remaining form an exclusive group which has its own group code. Only those who know the code are allowed to be members of the group. The group must now decide what their code is to be. They could select either a verbal or a physical code.

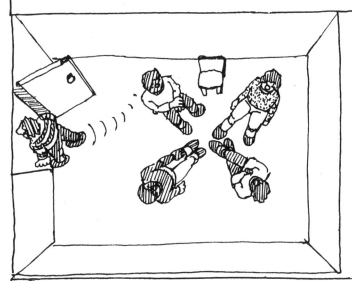

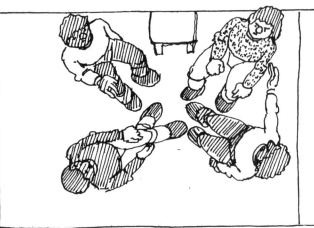

② The group discuss any subject eg music - clothes etc.

③   The 'outsider' now returns. By observing the group they try to identify the exclusive code. The 'outsider' must be ignored until they display the correct code.

I really enjoy their music

their latest is the best

I've got it! everyone has to look at Jayne before speaking.

④ Once the 'outsider' has worked out the code they are accepted into the group. Someone else takes a turn at being the outsider.

⑤   More complicated codes could include looking at one person and then crossing legs before talking. A verbal code might be to have the first word spoken in each exchange beginning with the same letter - although this can make conversation difficult.

The Auction

PART 1   Divide the group into separate units of three or four people in each. Each 'unit' is given an 'auction sheet' which lists a number of personal attributes and ambitions all of which are to be sold in auction. Every unit is given 100 tokens/points which are to be used for making bids for one or more of the items on the auction sheet.

The bid sheet records which items are bid for and how much is bid

we all agree? OK we'll bid the maximum for the PM's job.

How about 10 years of good health?

What happens after 10 years?

item	bid
Ten years of good health	
high artistic ability	
high musical ability	
high sporting ability	
high academic ability	
a good secure job	
2 years paid leave	
good exam results	

item	bid
An adventure trip around the world	
good looks	
attractive personality	
a high IQ	
a happy marriage	

PART 2   Everyone comes together for the sale. Each item is sold to the unit which places the highest bid. If two units make the same bid for the same item it is shared.

each unit explains the reasons for the chosen bids.

This exercise can be adopted for use with team building and management groups. 'Sale' items might then include; good communication, efficient administration, good industrial relations, a bonus system etc.

Ship Wreck

① Ask the group to imagine that they have been shipwrecked and stranded on an island. They will be stuck there for years.

② We'll have to agree a set of rules to live by

and actions that are crimes

And a set of penalties to enforce them

③
Rules and crimes

no stealing food

no stealing clothes

no bullying ....etc

Penalties

drowning

exile for a week etc.

do work for the others

④ The rules and penalties should be arranged in order of importance. The group should consider which penalty is most appropriate to each rule if broken. Discussion points may include - Who do the rules protect? Why is one rule more important than another? What do the penalties achieve? Why have rules?

Lucky Dip

① A number of everyday items have been placed one in each of these cardboard boxes. One person is blindfolded. They must feel for the object in a box and describe it to the rest of the group (without naming it if they guess what it is.) The rest of the group attempt to name the object.

only the instructor can see the object

The group face away from the boxes

② Start here

It's a flat oblong shape.. it feels rubbery..

③ It's hard and bent in the middle into a "V" shape .....

Is it a boomerang?

Telephone Pictures 1

Telephone Pictures 2

① In this version the 'director' must describe to the 'drawers' an object without naming it.

Only the director can see the object

The 'drawers' attempt to recreate the image.

② The objects to be described should be constructed from geometric shapes

put a semi circle on top ......

③ Only geometric terms can be used to describe the object eg. circle - dot etc. NOT eye, nose etc.

put 3 dots in a line down the middle of .. ..

Blindfold Maze 1

① A maze is created on grass using string tied around stakes. Balloons have been attached at intervals around the course. The group is divided into two opposing teams. Team A will attempt to burst all the balloons. Team B will try to prevent them.

② Two persons from each team are blindfolded (the robots) Each pair of 'robots' enters the maze from opposite sides. The 'robots' are directed by their seeing team mates. Team B robots, the 'chasers', try and 'tag' Team B robots, the 'bursters'. Once tagged the robots leave the maze and are replaced by new robots.

Blindfold Maze II

① In two opposing teams. Both teams attempt to retrieve the box which is located in the centre of the maze by directing a blindfolded robot. The Maze is guarded by a blindfolded guard robot who comes complete with its own independent seeing director.

robots

independent 'guard' director

The guard robots must not enter the shaded area

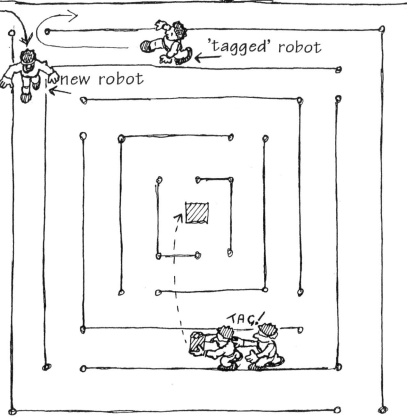

② When a robot is tagged they must leave the maze and cannot return. If the robot has picked up the box when tagged, the box is returned to the centre.

an alternative 'seeing' guard on a 'moon hopper'

'tagged' robot

new robot

TAG!

Problem Solving

Logic, Ingenuity and Imagination are required to resolve the problems in this section. Teamwork is also an important element particularly in 'Construction' (page 41) 'Cascade' (page 53) and 'Drawbridge' (page 57).

The problem entitled 'Balancing Act' (page 60) seems impossible to resolve at first sight. I am told that it has been around for some time but I have to admit that I hadn't seen it before. The solution is both simple and ingenious and it is well worth collecting the 20+ nails and a piece of wood in order to include it in a series of problem solving tasks.

Cloud Burst

Observation Game

① This activity is a test of memory and observation. It is simple to organise and is a good lead in to the more complex 'construction' exercise (next page) and also for 'Saboteur' (page 87) Participants are allowed 1 minute each to view and memorize a room and its contents.

The clock is set to the wrong time

② After viewing the room the group must answer 10 questions.

1   How many desks are there ?

2   What time did the clock on the wall say ?

3   Which litter bin contained litter ?

4   What colour top was the person seated at the desk wearing ?

5   How many 'phones were there ?

                etc

Alternatively the group name 20 items in the room.

③ Outdoor variations on the same theme: 30 seconds are allowed to memorize:

A.   10 objects selected at random

B.   features on a landscape

① I have put together a structure using scaffolding poles. I have also made a diagram of the structure.

② The group are asked to inspect the structure. They are not provided with any measuring or recording equipment so they must memorize its dimensions.

SAFETY NOTE:
hard hats and shoes must be provided for
this activity.

continued ..

Construction I

③ Inspection time is up. The structure must now be passed through a section of drain pipe that has been suspended from a tree etc.

④ The structure must be dismantled and reconstructed

⑤ When the structure has been reassembled it is checked for accuracy against my original diagram.

Construction II

① This version of construction utilises items of camping and walking equipment which have been set out in a pattern and recorded on my diagram. The group inspect the 'campsite' and memorize the layout.

I'll memorize the items on this sleeping mat.

② All items of equipment from the campsite must be passed through the drain pipe and re-assembled in the same pattern at the new camp site.

Make the task difficult by making the new campsite more remote and setting time limits.

Five Minute Puzzles

Bridge the gap between two glasses (etc) using only a Five or Ten Pound Note (or similar size piece of paper). Balance at least 4 one pound coins in the middle of the note.

Place 10 different objects all begining with the same letter eg. 'S', inside a box of matches - No live creatures allowed.

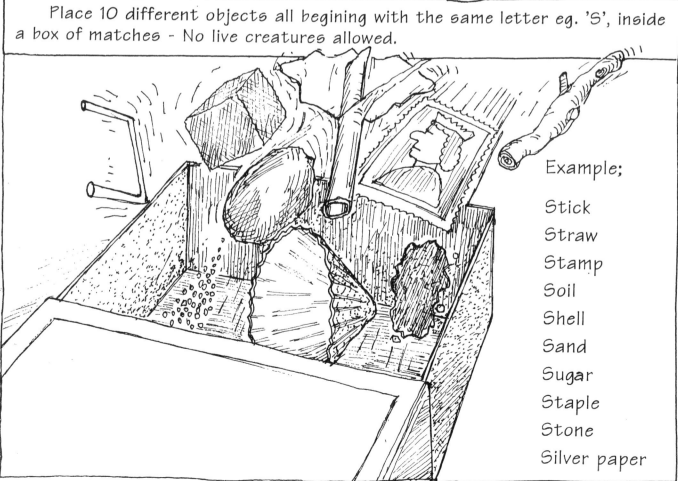

Example;

Stick
Straw
Stamp
Soil
Shell
Sand
Sugar
Staple
Stone
Silver paper

Postmans Walk

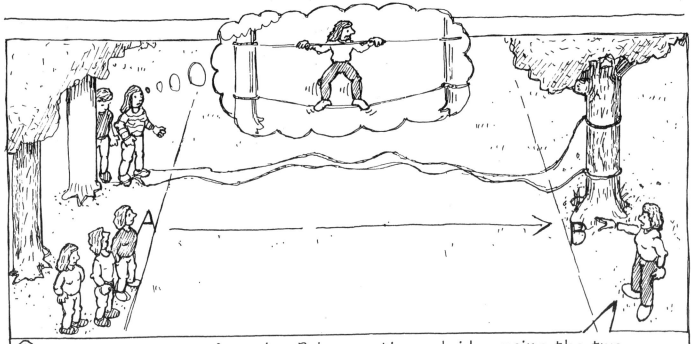

① You must cross from A - B by creating a bridge using the two ropes that have been tied to a tree on this side.

② The ground in between has been - mined - electrified - is full of sharks etc. Anybody who touches this area will be eliminated.

③

I have pre-tied 2 ropes to a tree on the opposite bank to the group using bowline knots. The groups are supplied with 4 climbing slings and 6 karabiners.

continued ..

Postmans Walk

④ A system to tension the rope bridge must be devised in order to prevent it from touching the ground when someone crosses it.

⑤

figure of eight knot

karabiner

ditto

slings and karabiners

tie off

⑥ ensure that all anchorage points are sound.

Swing Bridge

① Cross from A to B without touching the ground in between. You have 20 minutes planning time to walk around and examine the equipment.

Car tyre suspended from tree

A

1   2   x 2   oil drums   3   4   B

A scaffolding plank, just long enough to bridge the 4 equal distant gaps.

② The plank is too heavy for anyone sitting on the tyre to hold on to by just one end. So bridging gap No3 is going to be a problem.

③

④ Planning time is over. You have one attempt to get across.

continued ...

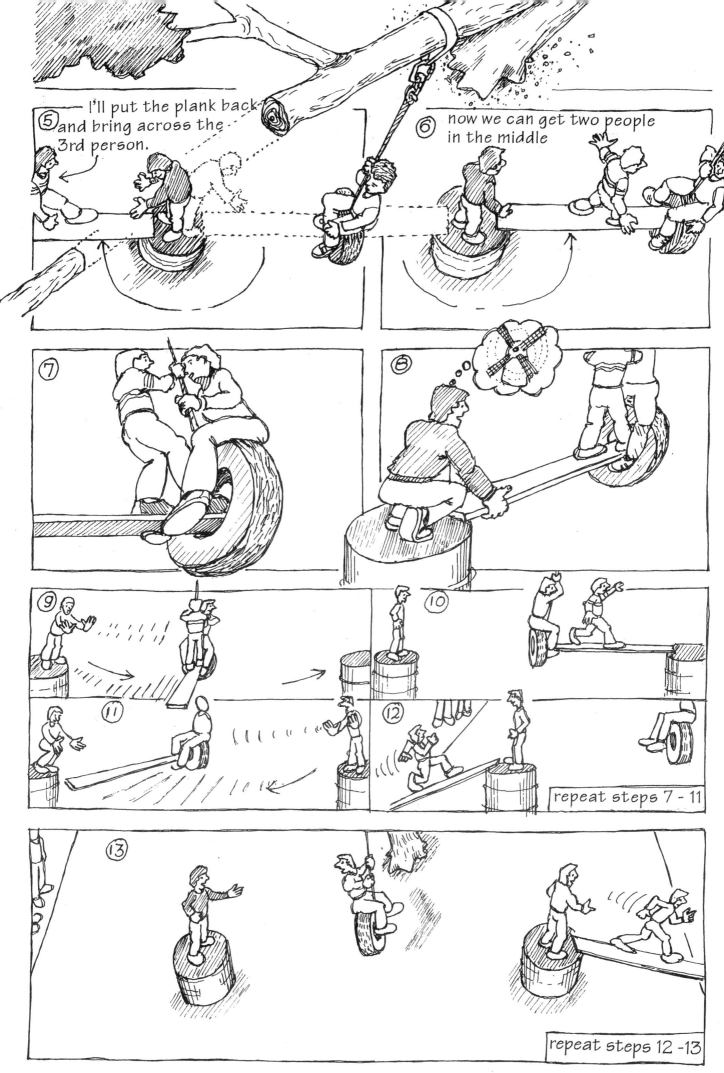

The Quest For Page 50

The Quest for Page 50

continued .....

Continued on page 120

Quicksand

Cascade

Cascade

Ravine

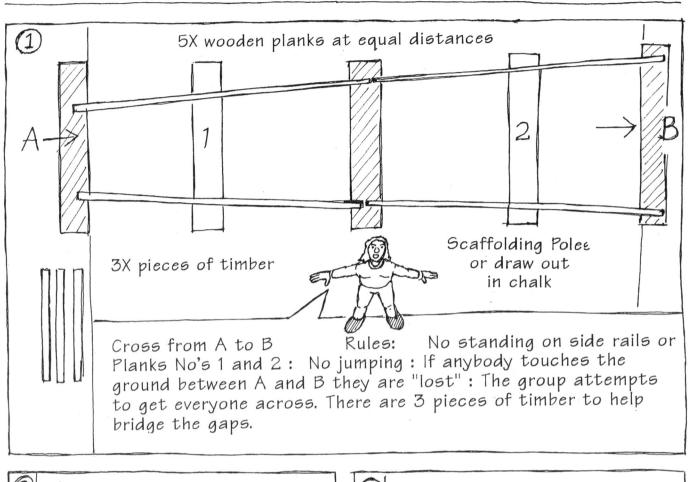

5X wooden planks at equal distances

A → 1 2 → B

3X pieces of timber

Scaffolding Poles or draw out in chalk

Cross from A to B   Rules: No standing on side rails or
Planks No's 1 and 2 : No jumping : If anybody touches the
ground between A and B they are "lost" : The group attempts
to get everyone across. There are 3 pieces of timber to help
bridge the gaps.

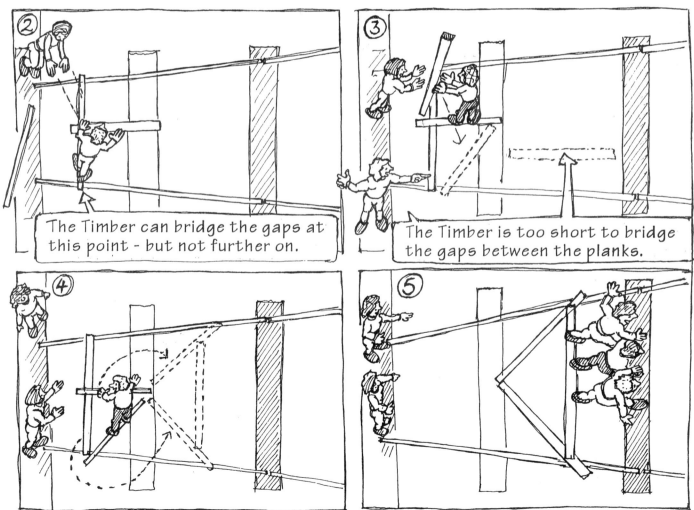

The Timber can bridge the gaps at this point - but not further on.

The Timber is too short to bridge the gaps between the planks.

Ravine

One person must return
to bring across the rest of the group

Drawbridge

① Cross the shallow stream, or marked out area, without walking through the water. One person is already on the opposite bank.

There are 3 strong wooden poles. Two of the poles should be equivalent in length to approximately 2/3 rds of the width of the stream.

x1 rope   X 3 poles   X 3 rope pieces

② ③

④ pull   ⑤ pull   ⑥ lower   ⑦

continued·····

57

Drawbridge

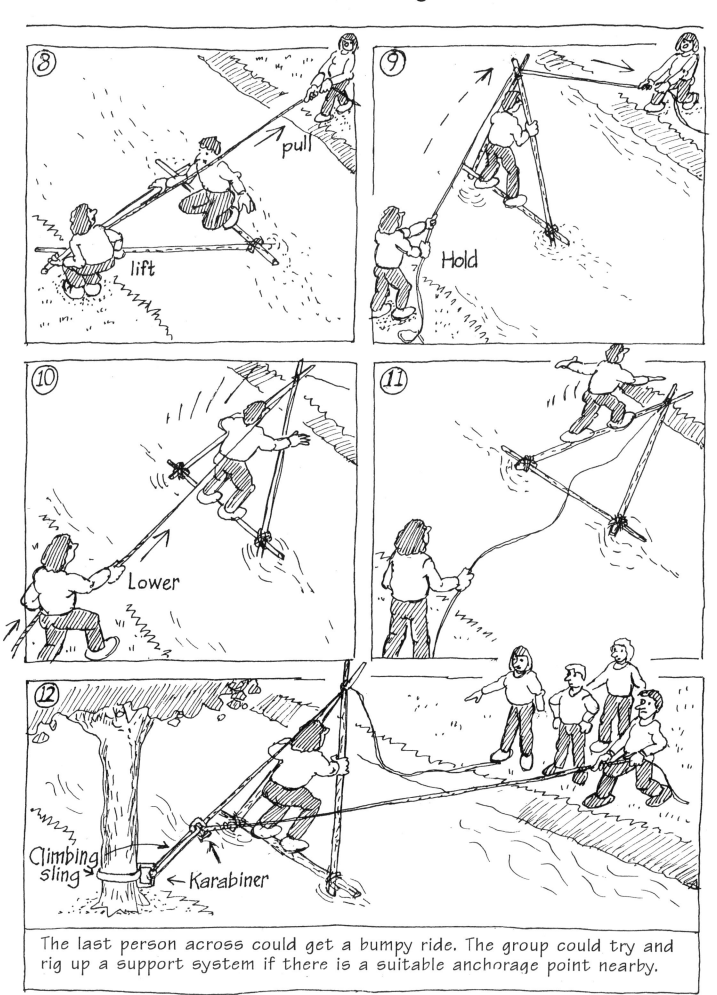

The last person across could get a bumpy ride. The group could try and rig up a support system if there is a suitable anchorage point nearby.

Rope Traverse

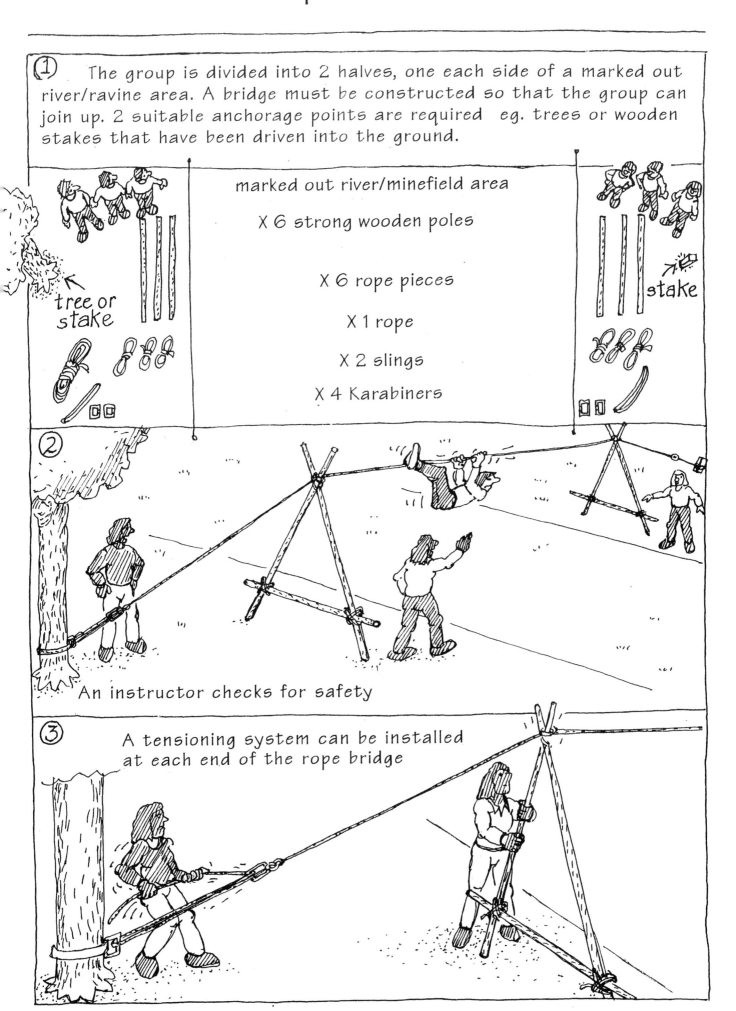

①   The group is divided into 2 halves, one each side of a marked out river/ravine area. A bridge must be constructed so that the group can join up. 2 suitable anchorage points are required   eg. trees or wooden stakes that have been driven into the ground.

marked out river/minefield area

X 6 strong wooden poles

X 6 rope pieces

X 1 rope

X 2 slings

X 4 Karabiners

tree or stake

stake

② An instructor checks for safety

③   A tensioning system can be installed at each end of the rope bridge

Balancing Act

① Balance all the loose nails on the top of the fixed nail head. The structure of nails must not make contact with anything other than each other and the fixed nail head.

20+ 4" flat head nails

4" flat head nail fixed into a wooden block

wooden block

②

③

④

⑤

It is possible to balance at least 24 nails by adding extra nails to the structure when in place. Even greater numbers can be balanced if 6" nails are used.

Floater

Floater 2

White Water 1

① Cross the "rapids" using the 4 small islands as stepping stones (Square carpet tiles are ideal) and 3 wooden planks of equal length to bridge the gaps (Floor boards are easy to handle). One of the planks is on the bank and this must be retrieved before all the group can get across

SAFE AREA

RIVER AREA

② Arrange the square islands so that the gaps at points 1 - 4 are just wider than the length of the planks. The planks can bridge the gaps at A, B and C.

SAFE AREA

③ No more than two people are allowed on any island at the same time and no jumping between islands

If anybody steps onto the river they are swept away and lost - alternatively apply point or time penalties or return to the start.

Continued ......

White Water 1

64

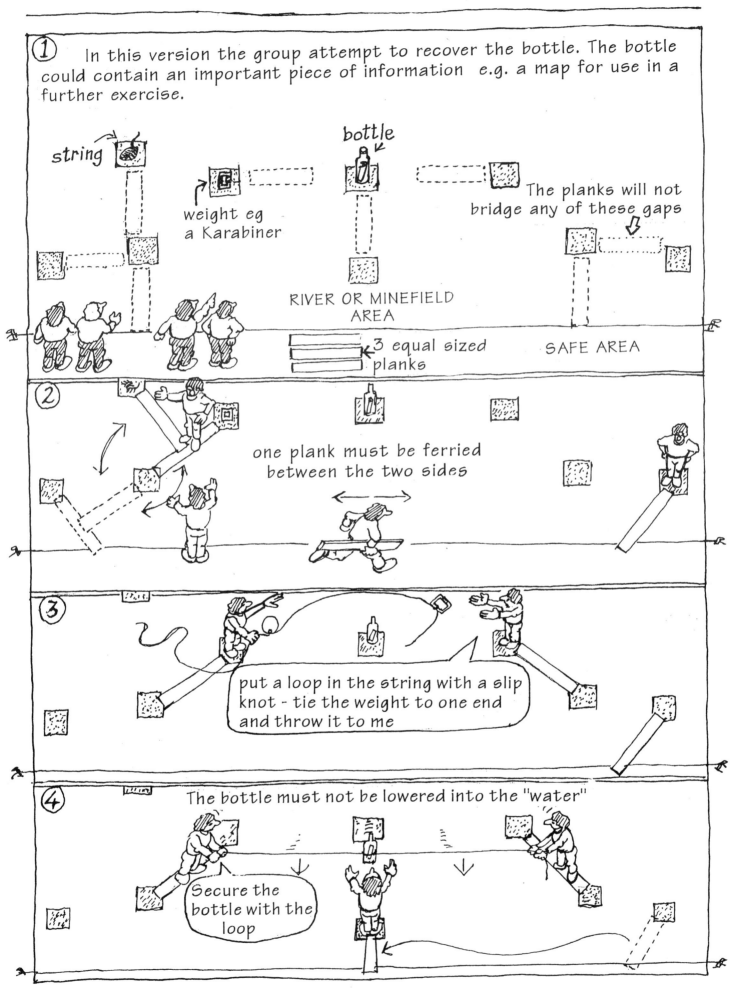

Fawlty Towers

① In small groups - construct a tower 5' in height using only newspapers and **sellotape** within a time limit of half an hour. The relative strength of each tower is tested when the time is up. Each tower must be capable of supporting a container.

② ③ ④ 1-2-3.... ⑤ 22-23-24 24!

A container is placed on the top of each completed tower. Marbles are then added, one at a time, to see which tower will support the most marbles before collapsing.

Fawlty Bridges

This time small groups put together a newspaper structure which extends horizontally from the side of a table. It must not be in contact with the floor. The structure which extends furthest from the table without collapsing wins.

The Breakfast Puzzle

A considerable amount of analysis and persistance is required to work out the answer to this. Each person is given a pen and paper and a copy of the problem as laid out on the following page (This may be photocopied) Information may be passed around the group. The solution to this puzzle is provided in the grid below.

Home Town:	Coventry	Edinburgh	Keswick	Swansea	Neath
Door Colour:	Yellow	Blue	Red	Ivory	Green
Drink:	Water	Tea	Milk	Orange Juice	Coffee
Sport:	Football	Tennis	Swimming	Rugby	Hockey
Eat:	Toast	Eggs	Cereals	Porridge	Bread Rolls

The Breakfast Puzzle

You have taken a holiday job as a waiter/waitress in a hotel. Your task is to deliver the correct breakfast to the residents in Five different rooms. The rooms are in a line along the same corridor. Unfortunately there are no room numbers so you will have to work out who has ordered which breakfast from the following information ....

1. The people from Keswick are in the room with the red door

2. The people from Swansea have porridge

3. Coffee goes to the room with the green door

4. The people from Edinburgh have tea

5. The room with the green door is immediately to the right of the room with the ivory door

6. The people who swim in the morning have cereals

7. The people who play football are in the room with the yellow door

8. Milk goes to the people in the middle room

9. The people from Coventry are staying in the first room on the left

10. The people who play tennis are in the room next to the people who have ordered toast

11. The people who play football are in the room next to the people who have ordered eggs

12. The people who play rugby have ordered orange juice

13. The people from Neath play hockey

14. The people from Coventry are in the room with the yellow door

Question   who has ordered water and who has ordered bread rolls for breakfast ?

68

Pharaoh

① Retrieve the piece of wood without passing over or under the poles. You may handle the poles but the piece of wood must be within a triangle formed by the poles before you retrieve it.

3 poles etc.

object to be retrieved

②

③

④

Organisation

Organisational activities have much in common with those in the proceeding sections on problem solving and communication. They are separated here because more emphasis is placed on how the members of the group are working together. The task that is set in 'Get knotted' (page 83) can only be successfully completed if the group is well organised. 'Saboteur' (page 87) demonstrates how group dynamics can effect the overall performance in relation to achieving objectives. It is also a good problem solving activity. Other activities such as 'Dragons and Dragon Slayers' (page 89) and 'Cat and Mouse Tag' (page 80) are worth doing if only for the fun and enjoyment they can generate.

Spot Light

① Divide the group into a number of smaller units. Each unit is given a number of playing cards - one for each person. The playing cards must be of the same value for each unit. The object is for each unit to try and score the highest number of points (the value of each card) by taking their cards to a marked out "target" area eg. the top of a hill without being "spotted". The "target" area is defended by a guard.

Target area

The guard is equipped with a torch

The guard is not allowed to enter the target area or to keep the torch switched on for more than 3 seconds.

If anyone is caught in the spotlight they are 'eliminated'

② Each unit is allowed time to plan a strategy

You take all the cards and we'll create a diversion so that you can get through !

Lets share out the cards at random.

Spot Light II

In Spot Light II the members of each unit are dropped off individually at different points away from their target area. Each person is provided with a map which indicates their position and that of the target. Everyone must make their own attempt on the target. The units are first allowed planning time to decide how to share out cards before they are dropped off.

You're the best navigator so you take the King.

Target area

guard

Review note: were the decisions about who to give the high scoring cards born out in practice?

Contract Orienteering

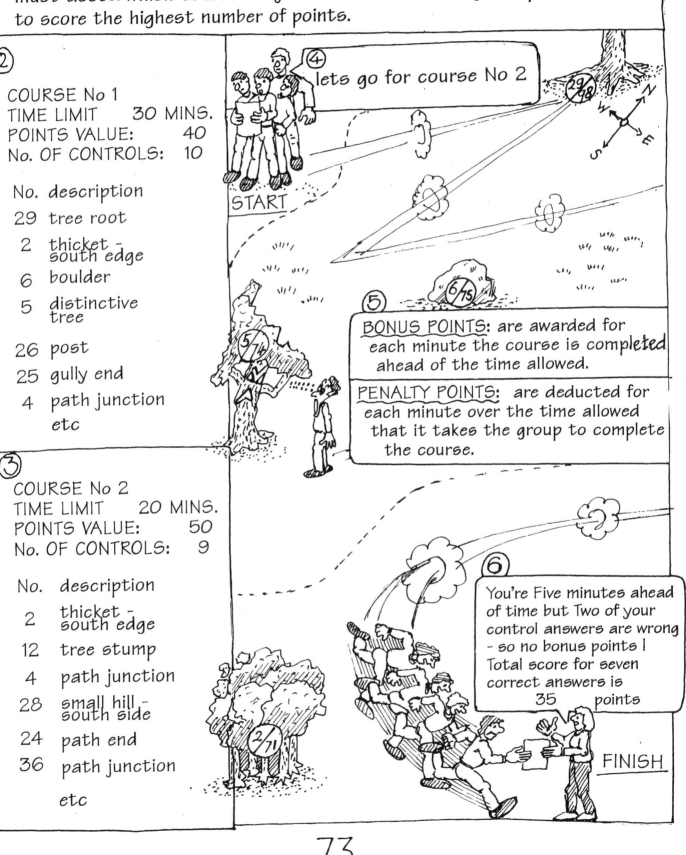

① The group is given a standard orienteering map. Instructions are provide for 2 or more different courses of varying degrees of difficulty relating to: distance, time limits and the number of control points that must be visited. Each course is given a different points value. The group must assess which course they can most realistically complete in order to score the highest number of points.

② COURSE No 1
TIME LIMIT   30 MINS.
POINTS VALUE: 40
No. OF CONTROLS: 10

No.	description
29	tree root
2	thicket - south edge
6	boulder
5	distinctive tree
26	post
25	gully end
4	path junction
	etc

④ lets go for course No 2

START

⑤ BONUS POINTS: are awarded for each minute the course is completed ahead of the time allowed.

PENALTY POINTS: are deducted for each minute over the time allowed that it takes the group to complete the course.

③ COURSE No 2
TIME LIMIT   20 MINS.
POINTS VALUE: 50
No. OF CONTROLS: 9

No.	description
2	thicket - south edge
12	tree stump
4	path junction
28	small hill - south side
24	path end
36	path junction
	etc

⑥ You're Five minutes ahead of time but Two of your control answers are wrong - so no bonus points! Total score for seven correct answers is
    35   points

FINISH

73

Contract Orienteering Plus

In this version of contract orienteering a problem solving activity has been added to each of the different courses. This problem must be resolved in order to reach one of the control points. If the number from this control point is recovered it is worth an additional 10 points. Bonus and Penalty points apply as before.

Lake Perimeter Survey

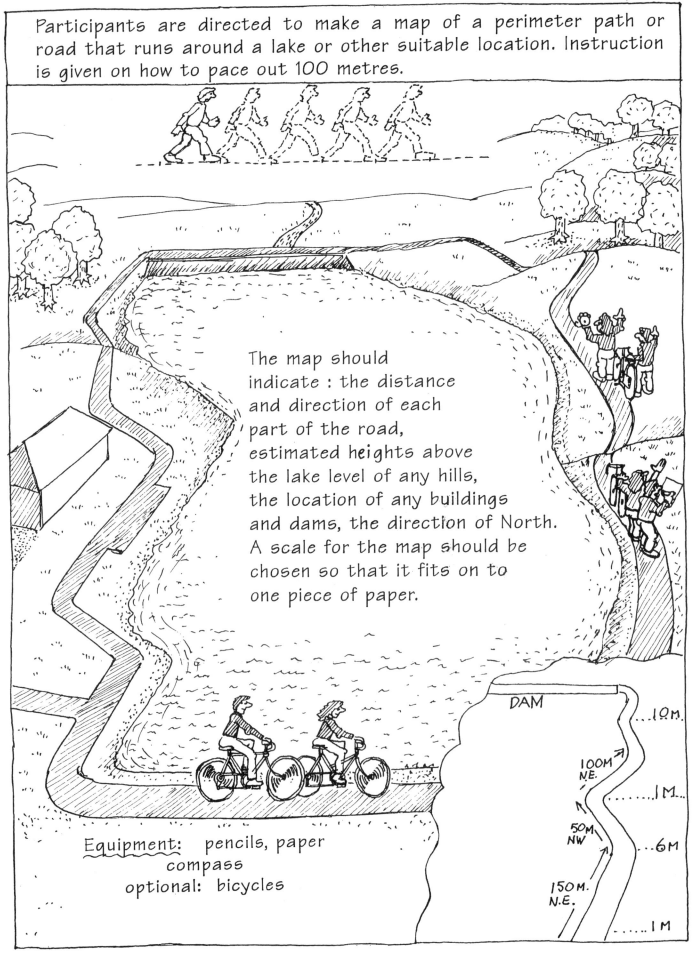

Participants are directed to make a map of a perimeter path or road that runs around a lake or other suitable location. Instruction is given on how to pace out 100 metres.

The map should indicate : the distance and direction of each part of the road, estimated heights above the lake level of any hills, the location of any buildings and dams, the direction of North. A scale for the map should be chosen so that it fits on to one piece of paper.

DAM

10M.

100M. N.E.

1M.

50M. NW

6M.

150M. N.E.

1M.

Equipment: pencils, paper
            compass
   optional: bicycles

Island Hopping

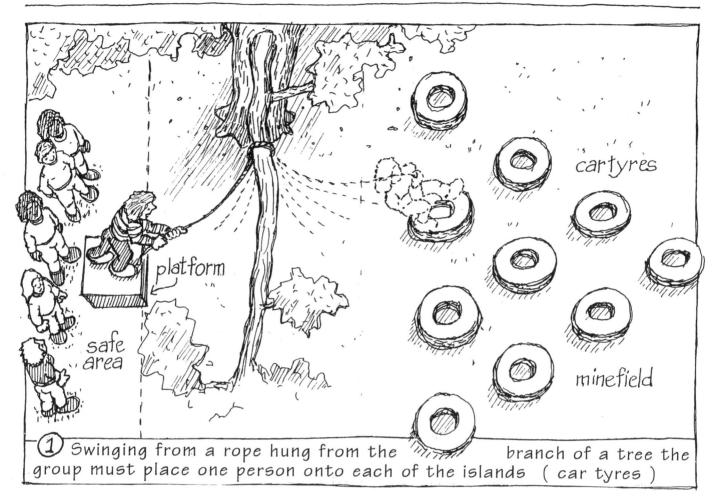

① Swinging from a rope hung from the branch of a tree the group must place one person onto each of the islands (car tyres)

② Stepping from one tyre to another is not allowed. Individuals can only be passed across to empty tyres.

If anyone steps on the minefield area they must return to the start.

Arrow Head

10 people standing in an arrow head formation. They must make the arrow point in the opposite direction with only 3 people moving their position.

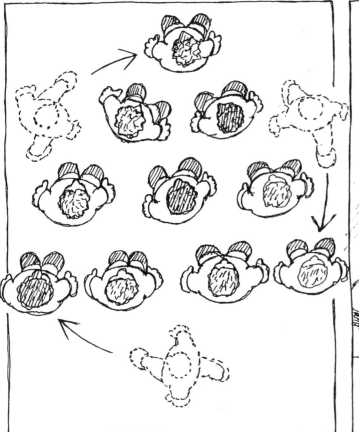

An easier alternative using car tyres and any size group.

Out of Line

1 Each person is given a number from 1 - 8. They must arrange themselves in the pattern of car tyres or similar without any consecutive numbers being next door either in a line across or diagonally.

no consecutive No's in any direction

x8 car tyre etc.

2 If there are fewer than 8 in the group make up the numbers by placing cards in the spare places. If there are more than 8 the extra people stand on the side and help direct the others.

3

78

Square Puzzle

① Draw a grid in chalk as illustrated. 8 people are asked to stand one in each of the outer squares

② Each person is given a numbered card, 1 - 8 at random

④ They must arrange themselves in numerical order ...

⑤ Individuals may move sideways and up or down into empty squares. No diagonal moves are allowed. Only one person at a time is allowed to occupy a square.

1	2	3
4	5	6
7	8	

Cat and Mouse Tag

①   A game of chase for larger groups. One person is selected to be the 'cat' and another to be the mouse. A 3rd person is selected to be the 'caller'. The rest of the group stand in the formation illustrated. Select another pair to be cat and mouse when the mouse is 'tagged'

② The caller stands with their back to the group.

③   Go! the 'cat' chases the 'mouse' along the avenues created by the group. They must NOT break through the arms.

④ at intervals the caller shouts 'change'

change !

⑤ Each person in the formation makes a 90° turn left.

change !

80

The Organisation Game

The group aim to score at least 200 points by completing a range of tasks within a time limit. Each task has been allocated a points value which is awarded to the group when they have successfully completed it. The tasks may be completed in any order but it is advisable to read the whole list first. If you are working with a very impetuous group get them to complete 'The Three Minute Quiz' on page 21 before starting this exercise. (200 points can only be achieved if the bonus points are gained at the end of the task list)

The Task List

1   What would happen if you were to stand in a position 1.5 K. SW of this base ? - 15 points

2   At exactly 6pm get the whole group together and shout "we will succeed" - 25 points

3   Produce a bowline knot - 15 points

4   Give the 6 figure grid reference for this base - 10 points

5   Produce a Figure of Eight knot - 10 points

6   Produce an oak leaf - 10 points

7   What is the number of the 'phone box that is situated at the south end of Brideacre Gardens - 15 points

8   Put 10 objects all beginning with the same letter in a match box - 10 points (see page 44)

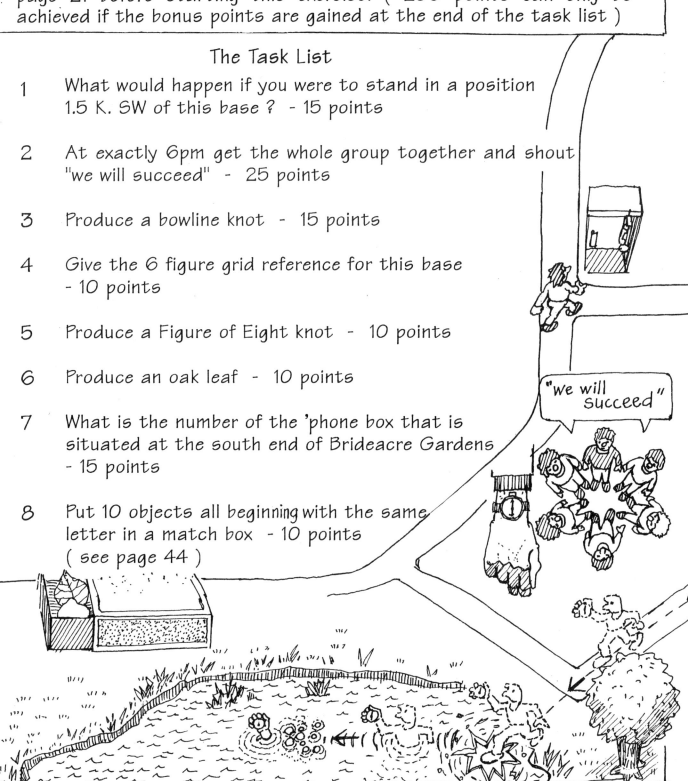

The Organisation Game

9   What is the number of the telephone box on the corner of Axholme Rd. ? - 15 points

10 Produce a correctly completed crossword from todays newspaper - 10 points

11 Carry one person safely around the building - 15 points

12 Produce a leaf from the lava tree - 20 points

13 Bonus for completing No 7 before No's 1 - 5 - 25 points

14 Bonus for answering No 9 within 10 minutes of going for the answer - 25 points

15 Bonus for completing No 8 within 10 minutes of starting - 10 points

Equipment list: compass - local OS map - rope/string - book of knots - small matchbox - todays newspaper

Get Knotted

① Three separate groups, A B and C, work together to try and connect 3 ropes using 5 different knots. The instructions on how to put the ropes together and various pieces of equipment are split between the different groups. Intergroup communication is passed around by an instructor. One hour is allowed to complete the task.

② There are various restrictions on how information and equipment is passed around.

Group A

Group A can only communicate with Group B

③ Post travels in one direction only A-B-C-A-B-C etc.

post

post

half hitch

bowline

figure of eight

reef knot

sheep shank

④ Letter post, ie Notes, travel direct. However parcel post, ie the ropes, must complete two circuits before I'll deliver them. I'll only pass on this information if they ask me !

Group C

green rope

Group C can only communicate with Group A

Group B

Book of Knots

Group B can only communicate with Group C

continued ...

Get Knotted

⑤ All of the separated information contained on the individual instruction lists must be shared before the task can be completed

⑥ Instruction List
for group A

Group B must tie the red rope to the green rope with a reef knot.

Group C must tie a figure of eight knot in the middle of the blue rope.

⑦ Instruction List
for group B

Group C must tie the red rope to the red rope with a bowline halfway between the reef knot and the half hitch.

⑧ Instruction List
for group C

Group A must tie the blue rope to the red rope with a half hitch.

Group A must tie the blue rope to the green rope with a sheep shank.

Scatter

Saboteur

① A structure of lettered cardboard boxes has been put together in a closed room. The group are given 1 hour to replicate the structure in another room using similar boxes. Only one person at a time is allowed to view the model structure, which must be memorised by the viewer. Each time the model is viewed 5 minutes is deducted from the groups construction time.

model structure

② The group is allowed time to plan before starting

③ The structure can only be viewed from one position on each visit.

④ The "clock" starts when they pick up the first box

Letter A goes here

no it doesn't

⑤ After starting the task each person is taken individually into a separate room and told ....

One person in your group MIGHT be a saboteur - but it isn't you !!

⑥ The group consider what they have all been individually told

It sounds like we have all been told the same thing

We can't be sure - no one is going to admit to being the saboteur

continued ....

Saboteur

Group A fail because they are deflected from the task by suspicion and argument, and lose time penalties by rechecking each others viewings.

Group B are not deflected by the unsubstantiated rumours of a saboteur and complete the structure. This exercise illustrates just how destructive suspicion and distrust can be to effective teamwork.

Dragons & Dragon Slayers

① In two opposing teams (Dragons Vs Dragon Slayers) dragons collect eggs (balloons) and tie them to the square. Dragon Slayers destroy eggs (burst balloons) and tie them to the same square. I've tied lots of balloons around the field.

Square of string tied around 4 tent pegs.

② RULES a, Dragons and Dragon Slayers may only carry one balloon at a time.
   b, If a Dragon has collected a balloon a Dragon Slayer may not burst it.

BANG!
BANG!
BANG!

③ Count up burst\un-burst balloons to determine winners.

Now here's a great game called Wizards and W...

SMASH!!

News Flash

① This team work exercise simulates a news team. 30 - 45 mins is allowed to prepare a news programme with each person given a specific task to perform. Lots of news paper cuttings are provided for the selection of news items.

② After about 20 mins insert a major news item which must be the lead story.

③ Here is the news

The programme must go out on time.

④ Create further pressure by presenting a news flash eg, The Prime Minister has resigned etc

⑤ The group watch the final product

Review notes

How were decisions made and news items selected? How did they cope working under pressure, and handle a crisis? How did they decide on the balance of news etc.

A-Z of Photography

Create a photographic representation of each letter of the alphabet using only members of the group and a camera. View the prints at the next session.

Personal Organisation

① Instruction is given about the basic principles of packing a rucksack for a walk in the hills, taking account of the prevailing weather conditions and forecasts. Each person is given a rucksack to pack with all the necessary equipment for an expedition in remote country.

② A simulated walk follows with the leader calling out instructions to illustrate the importance of careful packing.

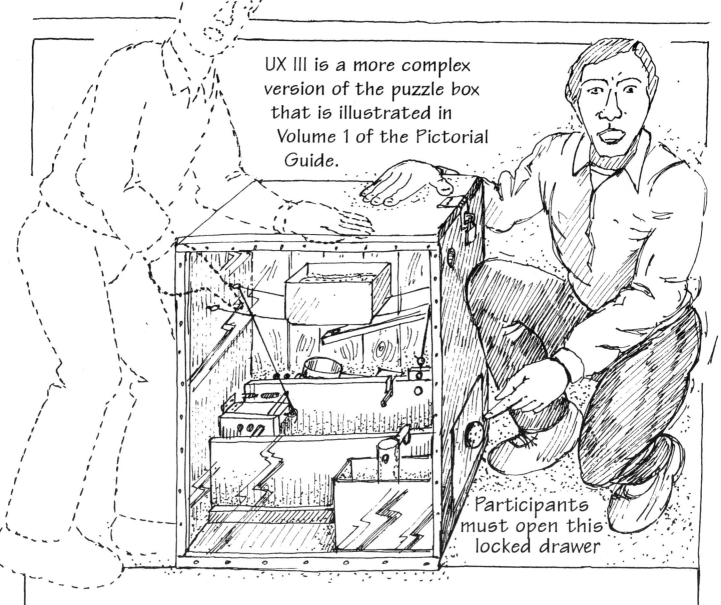

UX III is a more complex
version of the puzzle box
that is illustrated in
Volume 1 of the Pictorial
Guide.

Participants
must open this
locked drawer

.   This box has been produced with a clear perspex side through
which can be seen Four locking mechanisms. These prevent the drawer
at the bottom of the box from being opened. The locks are guarded
by a water trap. This is activated if either one of two locks is
incorrectly opened. Participants must work out from observation how
to unlock the drawer and retrieve whatever reward is being held in it.
All the items of equipment illustrated below are required to unlock
the box. The following pages illustrate how the box works.

wooden dowel

plastic
bottle &
water

bag of marbles

flexible
pipe

socket set

continued.....

UX III Super Box - 'The Quest'

UX III can be used in a variety of ways. In the 'Quest' it forms the centre piece of a series of problem solving activities. Each problem has to be resolved in order to recover various items of equipment. All of the equipment is needed to open the box.

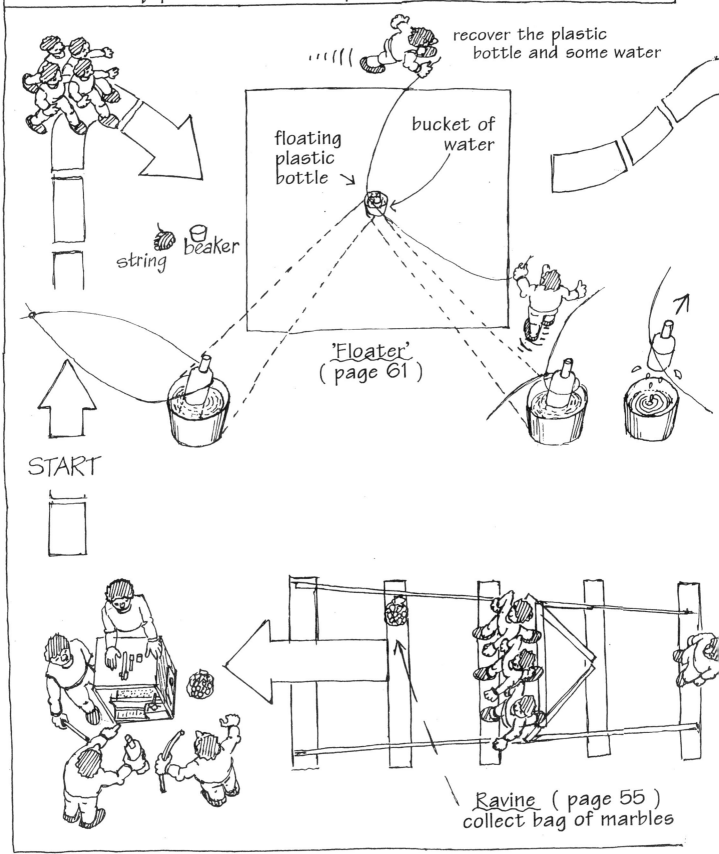

recover the plastic bottle and some water

floating plastic bottle

bucket of water

string   beaker

'Floater'
(page 61)

START

Ravine (page 55)
collect bag of marbles

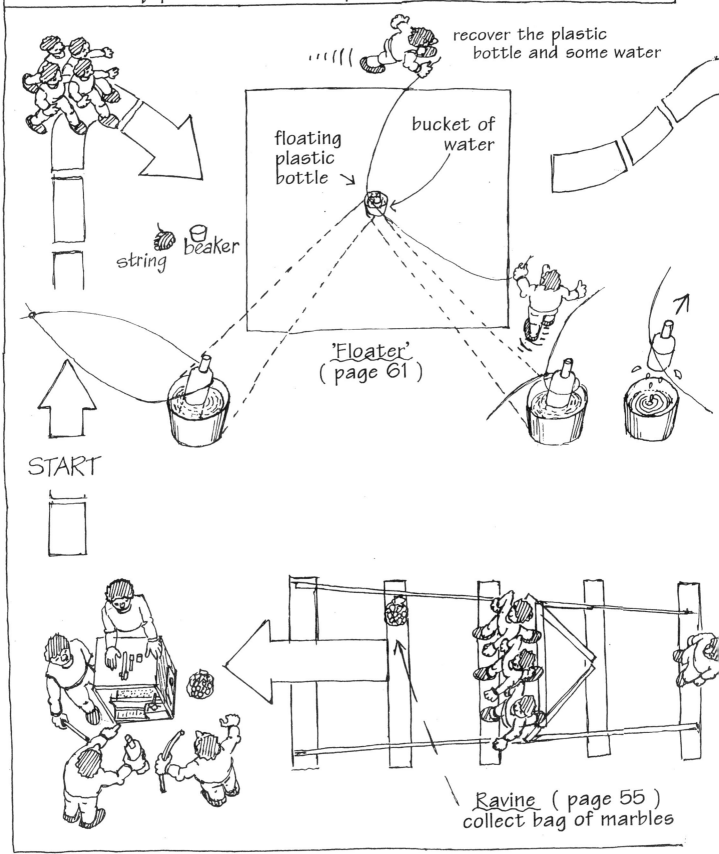

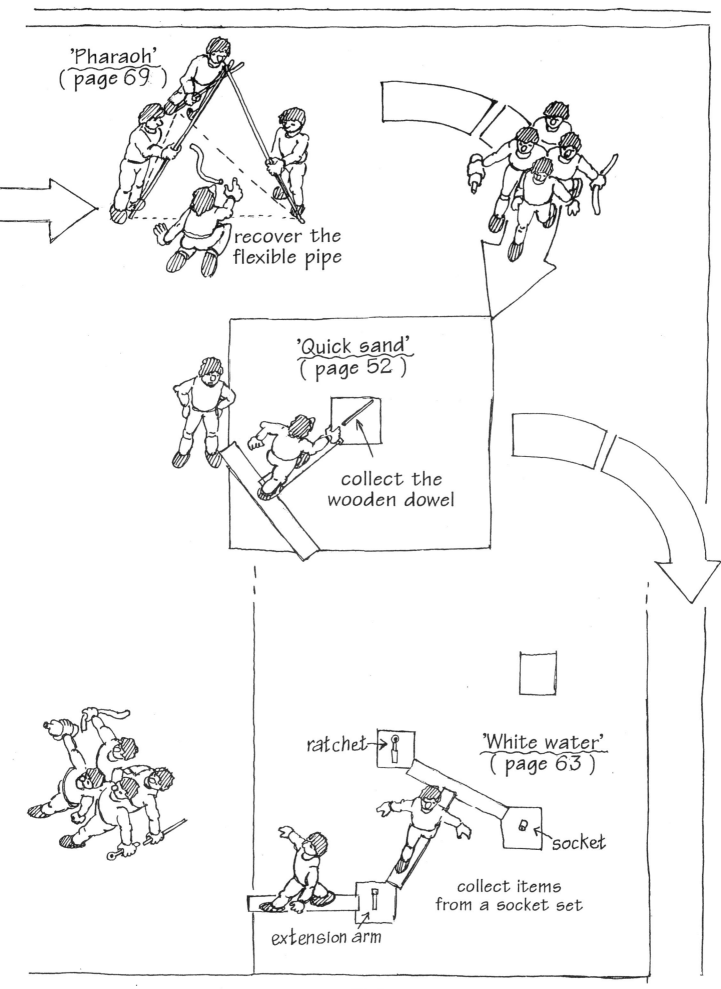

'Pharaoh'
(page 69)

recover the
flexible pipe

'Quick sand'
(page 52)

collect the
wooden dowel

ratchet →

'White water'
(page 63)

socket

collect items
from a socket set

extension arm

UX III Super Box
- The locking mechanisms

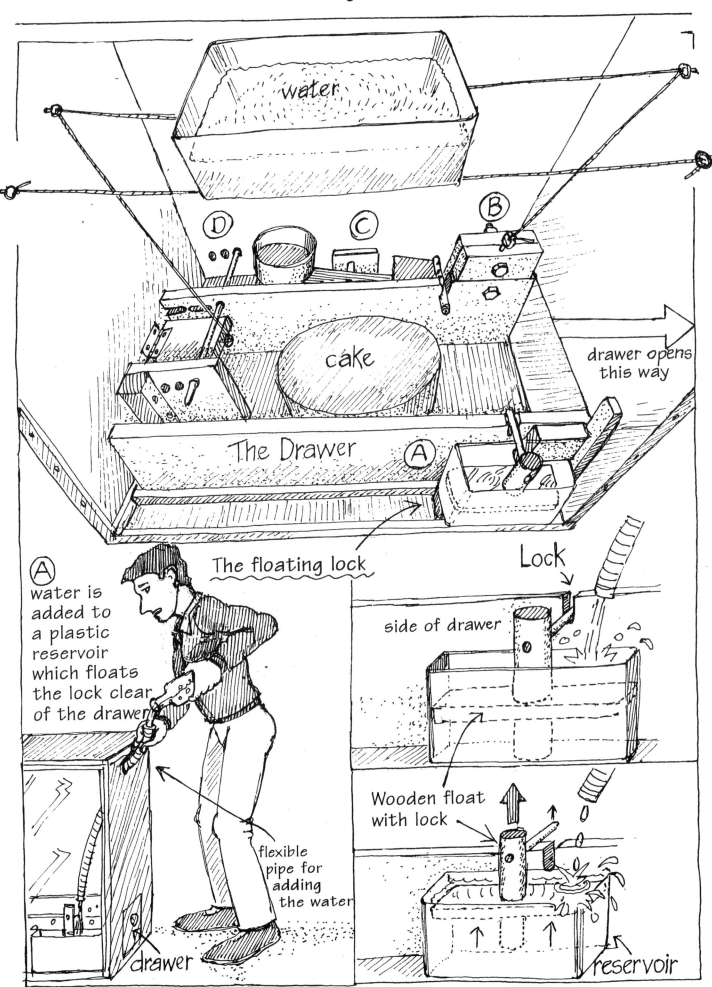

water

Ⓓ Ⓒ Ⓑ

cake

drawer opens
this way

The Drawer

Ⓐ

The floating lock

Ⓐ
water is
added to
a plastic
reservoir
which floats
the lock clear
of the drawer

flexible
pipe for
adding
the water

drawer

Lock

side of drawer

Wooden float
with lock

reservoir

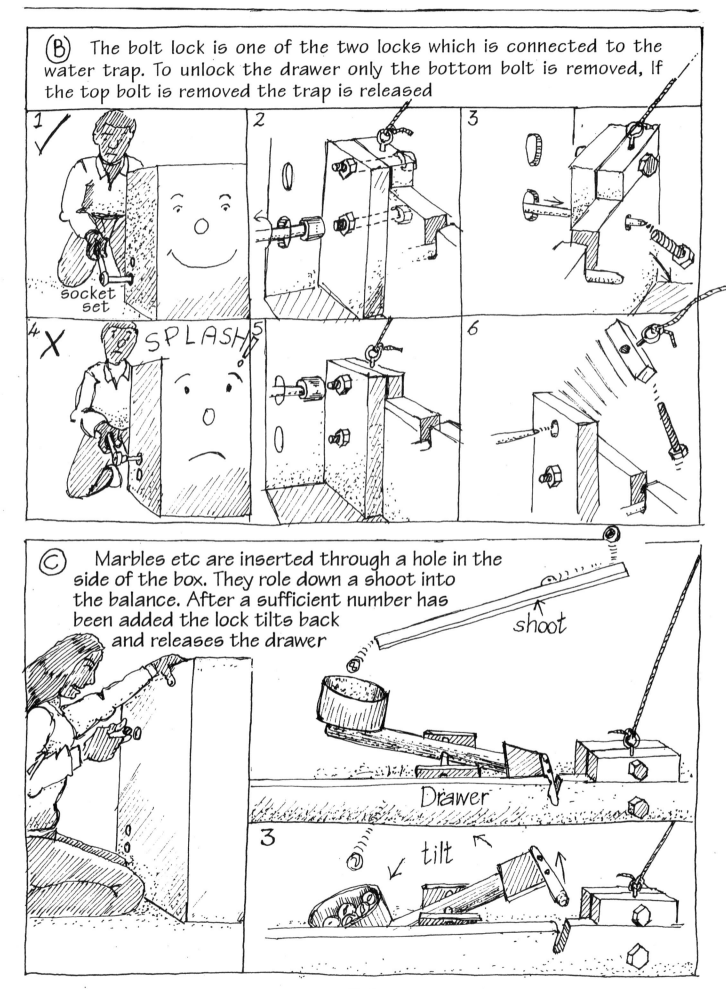

(B) The bolt lock is one of the two locks which is connected to the water trap. To unlock the drawer only the bottom bolt is removed, If the top bolt is removed the trap is released

1

socket set

2

3

4

SPLASH

5

6

(C) Marbles etc are inserted through a hole in the side of the box. They role down a shoot into the balance. After a sufficient number has been added the lock tilts back and releases the drawer

shoot

Drawer

3

tilt

UX III Super Box
- The <u>dowel lock</u> and <u>water trap</u>

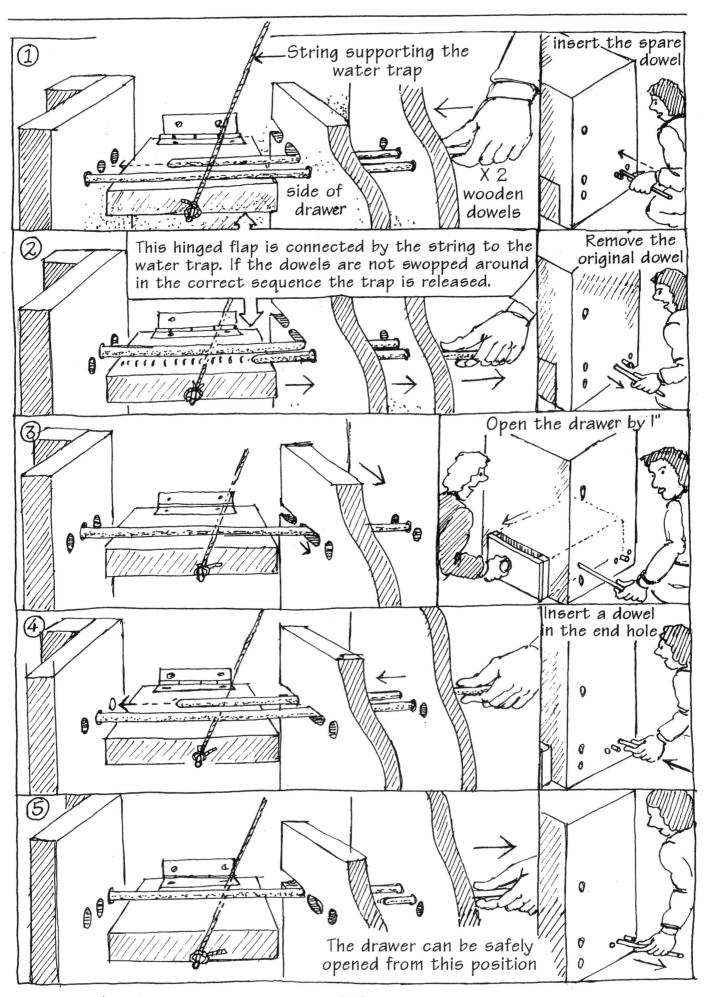

① String supporting the water trap

insert the spare dowel

side of drawer

X 2 wooden dowels

② This hinged flap is connected by the string to the water trap. If the dowels are not swopped around in the correct sequence the trap is released.

Remove the original dowel

③ Open the drawer by I"

④ Insert a dowel in the end hole

⑤ The drawer can be safely opened from this position

UX III Super Box

As an alternative to the sudden death approach when the water trap is released incorporate UX III into a points earning exercise. A points value is awarded after each problem is solved. Participants attempt to score the maximum points

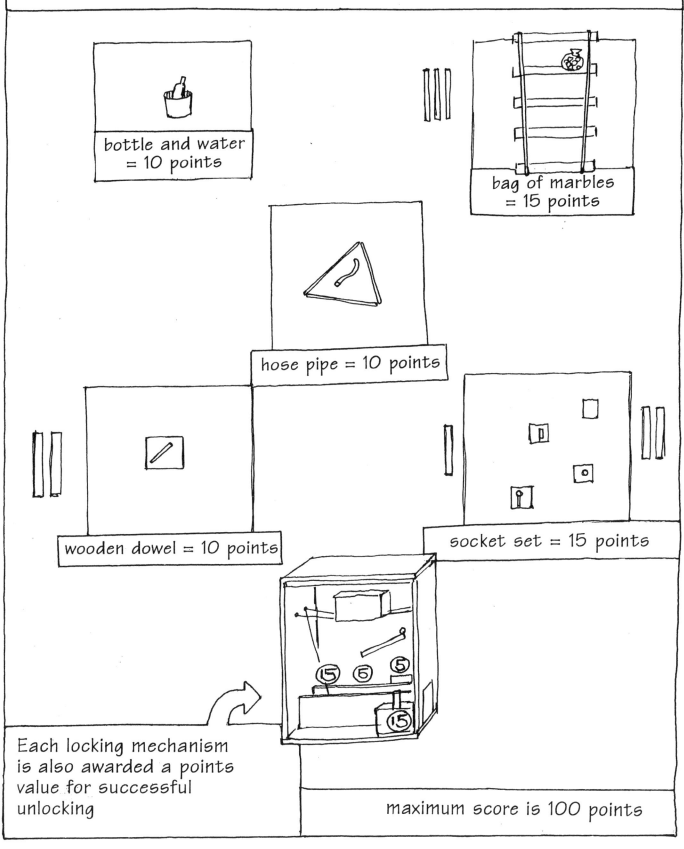

bottle and water = 10 points

bag of marbles = 15 points

hose pipe = 10 points

wooden dowel = 10 points

socket set = 15 points

Each locking mechanism is also awarded a points value for successful unlocking

maximum score is 100 points

UX III Super Box

see page 114 for the construction notes for UX III

Here are three alternative ways of employing the 'trap' mechanism and the consequences for failure

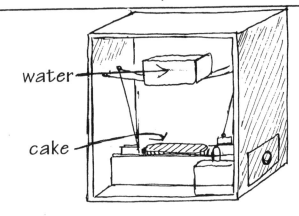

SPLASH!

water

cake

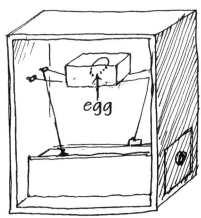

egg

SMASH!

An essential piece of information has been written on the egg so this must be retrieved without breaking it. This option avoids ruining a perfectly good cake if the trap is released.

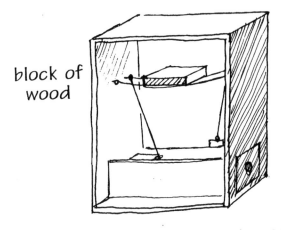
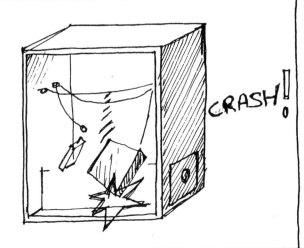

block of wood

CRASH!

In this version, each lock is given a points value which is awarded if it is successfully opened. If the trap is set off, loose 10 points etc.

Team Building

The following series of activities have been linked together to provide a full days event. I have run this and similar activities with large groups of 12+ although it can be simplified to run with smaller numbers. It is particularly useful in team building as it brings together all the key elements in teamwork eg. leadership - communication - decision making - organisation - sharing information - planning - evaluation etc. The event is divided into 4 distinct stages.

Stage I

Warm up exercise which includes dividing the group into 2 smaller units. This stage is fun and fairly easy. It enables the group to feel that they have achieved something and made a start. This is followed by a short debrief - how did they do - did everybody work together etc.

Stage II

This is a points earning exercise comprising lots of small problems to solve.

Stage III

The brief for the final stage IIII is given out. However, all the information has been fragmented. Participants must share all the pieces of information in order to make sense of the final stage. The points that were earned in the proceeding stage are used to 'buy' equipment that will be needed in the final stage.

Stage IIII

The two 'units' undertake an expedition collecting various items along the route. They will have to overcome a number of physical obstacles involving canoeing or climbing etc.

Final debrief.

Team Building stage I

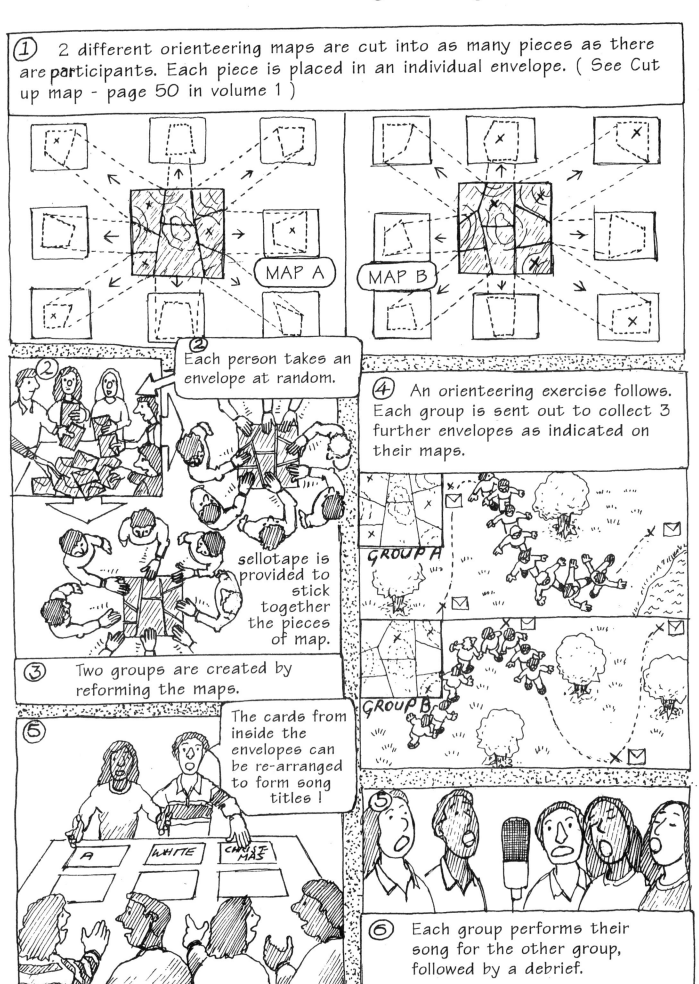

① 2 different orienteering maps are cut into as many pieces as there are participants. Each piece is placed in an individual envelope. (See Cut up map - page 50 in volume 1)

MAP A

MAP B

② Each person takes an envelope at random.

sellotape is provided to stick together the pieces of map.

③ Two groups are created by reforming the maps.

⑤ The cards from inside the envelopes can be re-arranged to form song titles !

A   WHITE   CHRIST-MAS

④ An orienteering exercise follows. Each group is sent out to collect 3 further envelopes as indicated on their maps.

GROUP A

GROUP B

⑥ Each group performs their song for the other group, followed by a debrief.

Team Building   stage II

⑦ The whole group is presented with a range of problem solving exercises. Each problem has been given a points value. eg ⟨5⟩   The object is to score as many points as possible within 1 hour. Points are used to buy various items of equipment that will be needed for the final stages. Add as many problems to the following examples as necessary.

Pharaoh

⟨10⟩

(page 69)

5 people complete the 3 minute test (page 21)

⟨5⟩

RING RING!

Give the compass bearings for 5 given landmarks

⟨5⟩

⟨10⟩

Throw the ball 3 times around the whole group without dropping it.

Floater (page 62)

⟨10⟩

Cascade (page 53)

⟨10⟩

⟨10⟩ Proceed to point X on the map. Telephone this No. – – – – – – Give the password 'ZORO' await the answer.

⟨5⟩

Quicksand (page 52)

Let's use this phone - it's much nearer - No one will know! TEE HEE!

ZORO!

OK, I'll call you back with the answer

Team Building   stage III

⑧ The brief is presented for the final stage. A set of instructions have been cut into as many separate pieces of information as there are participants Each piece is placed into an envelope and then handed out at random to every person. All the information must be shared and made sense if the group are to successfully complete the final stage.

Everybody must get across the river and meet at Grid ref .... by 5p.m.

Group B: collect equipment at river crossing

Group A: climb to 15 metres at Grid ref: ....

Group B: visit control No. 8 & collect equipment

Group A: cross the river at Grid ref: ....

Group B: collect equipment on island

Group B: visit control points No.s 2 and 12 collect equipment.

Group A: collect equipment when crossing river

Group B: collect information at control point No. 6

Group A: visit control points 30 and 31, collect equipment.

Group B: cross the river at Grid ref: ......

only climb or canoe under the supervision of the instructors

Group A: collect equipment at the top of 15 metre climb

Group B: canoe across lake

The lake crossing point is shown on control point No. 6

the river may only be crossed once

⑨ Both units must now decide what equipment to purchase using the points/tokens that they earned in the previous exercise. Not all the equipment is necessary. Here is a suggested equipment list: Compass, climbing ropes, safety harness, rucksack, torch, karabiners, orienteering maps, canoes, paddles, O.S. map etc.

⑩ The two sub groups are reformed. Each undertakes an expedition during which they recover various items of equipment that have been distributed around the course. In order to do this they must put together all of the information that was provided in stage III. They must also have purchased the 2 orienteering maps and 2 O.S. maps.

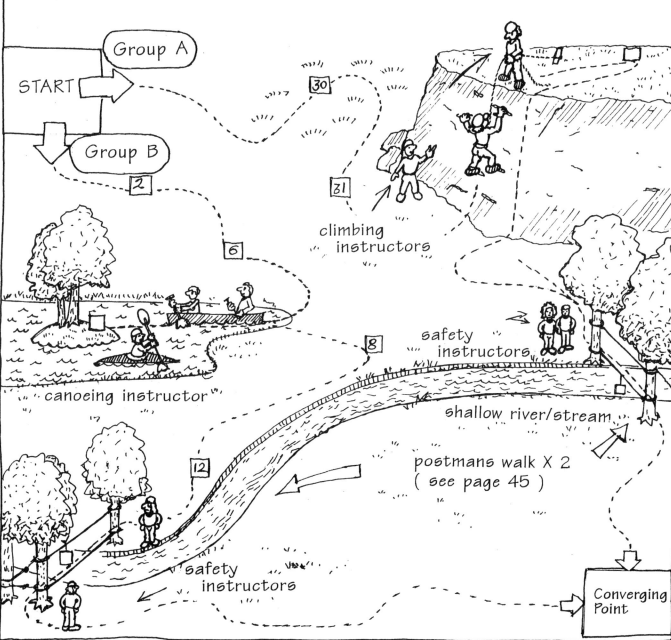

⑪ Fragmented information like a jigsaw has to be put together to provide a picture and knowledge. This may seem obvious but look at what happens after something goes seriously wrong either within an organisation or in the community. The inquiry into how the disaster happened reveals a failure by the responsible professionals to put together vital pieces of information and to take preventative action.

continued.......

Team Building IIII

⑫ If you do not have any access to suitable climbing or canoeing sites, problem solving activities can be substituted at key points during the expedition. eg. "white water' (page 63) , "Ravine" (page 55)

Once both of the units have reached the final destination following the expedition all of the components that should have been collected along the way are assembled. In this example the components make up a multi-element camping stove .....

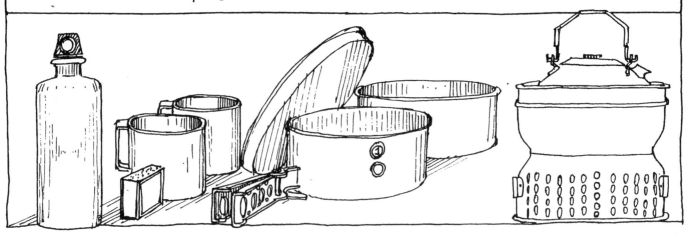

...... and the ingredients to make up a meal or some other suitable reward (eg mulled wine)

REVIEW NOTES: Was information shared, who did what - leaders, followers - how were decisions made, did the two units co-operate or compete etc.

PLAN.   DO.   REVIEW.

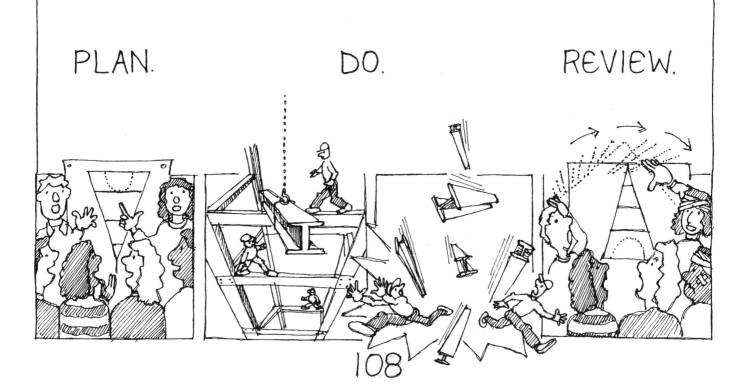

Group Sculpture

① Participants are asked to form a group sculpture to represent relationships using all members of the group. This can be done under the direction of one person or by the group collectively

② This is followed by a discussion about group dynamics - How can relationships be improved?

③ Are some individuals isolated?

④ Is conflict between subgroups undermining any shared objectives? etc.

Group Dynamics

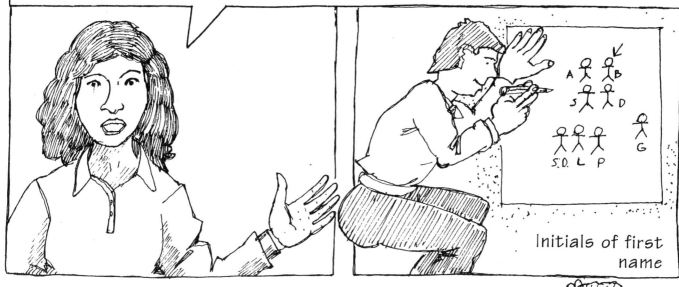

① As an alternative to group sculpture, individuals draw a diagram of their perception of group relationships using stick figures.

Initials of first name

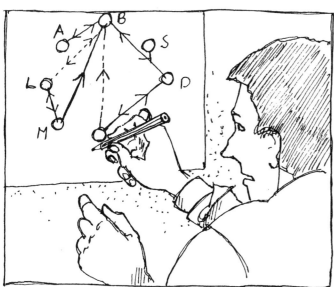

② In this version, each circle represents a member of the group. Lines are drawn between individuals who are considered to have strong relationships - the stronger the line the stronger the relationship. Arrows indicate whether it is a two way relationship etc.

110

Stairway to Heaven

Using a flip chart etc, draw two flights of stairs as illustrated. The group are asked to identify any negative attitudes or behaviour which are causing problems. These fill in the stairs downwards towards gloom and despondency. They are then asked to identify ways to improve their performance. Positive suggestions fill the stairs upwards towards light and achievement !

co-operate

share good ideas

talk and listen

As an alternative blank out the examples that have been shown on the stairs and photocopy the page. Each individual is handed a copy and they fill in their own ideas. These are then shared with the whole group.

arguments

too aggressive

selfish

don't listen

The Brick Wall

This is a variation on the previous exercise. This time the concept is progress along a road towards a shared objective. The way is barred by a brick wall. Participants suggest which aspects of group behaviour are creating obstacles to working together successfully. A discussion follows on what can be done to overcome the barriers that are created by negative attitudes or behaviour etc.

This exercise can be done using a flip chart or blank out the examples in the wall and photocopy for individual use.

Clockwork Review

① Divide the group into two circles facing each other in pairs. Each pair is told to spend two or three minutes discussing what they have liked about a recent activity or the overall course.

② After two or three minutes, the people in the inner circle are asked to move one position to face the next person in the outer circle. They now spend 2/3 minutes talking about what they disliked.

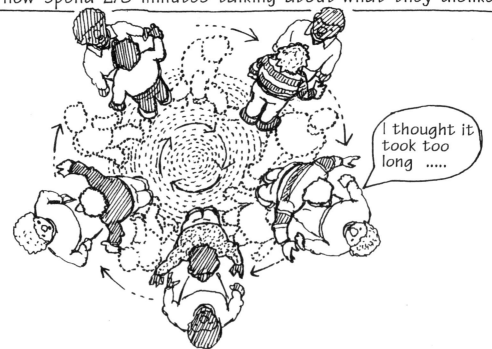

③ This procedure continues until a full circuit has been completed. Other discussion topics may include: suggestions for improving the course; the most challenging aspect; what have you learned etc.

UX 3 Construction Notes

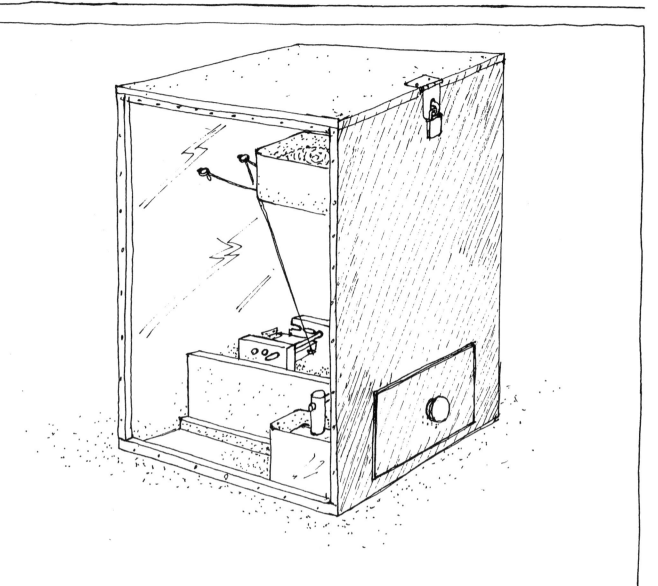

The construction of 'UX 3' is fairly simple and none of the individual locking elements are very complicated. It can be put together with carpentry equipment using basic materials and everyday items. A certain amount of trial and error is required to ensure that all the locks are reliable. The following notes show designs that I have found were efficient. There are numerous variations and additions that can be made to a puzzle box. All you need is some time and imagination.

UX3 Construction Notes

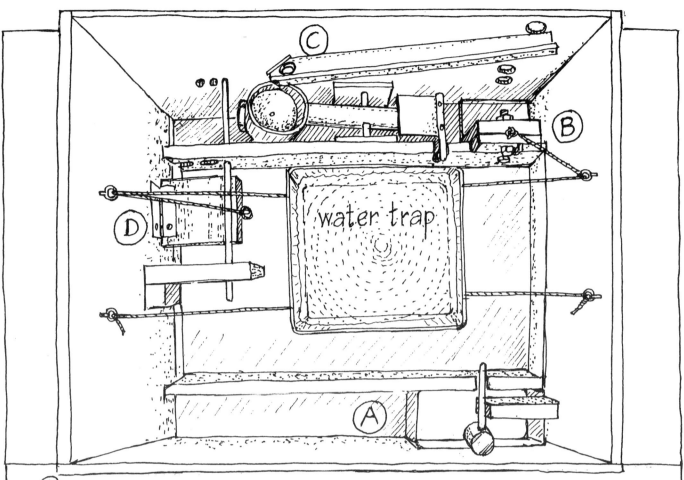

C

B

D

water trap

A

Ⓐ The 'Floating Lock" After several failed attempts at producing a locking devise that could be relied upon to unlock when the reservoir is filled with water I found that this design worked consistently.

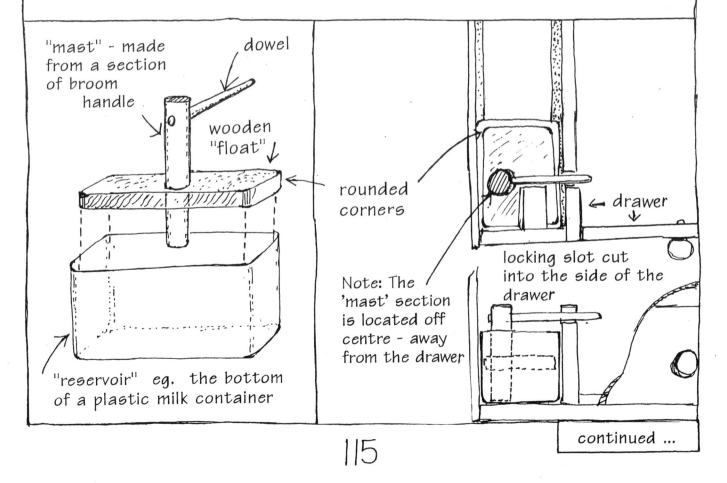

"mast" - made from a section of broom handle

dowel

wooden "float"

rounded corners

reservoir" eg. the bottom of a plastic milk container

Note: The 'mast' section is located off centre - away from the drawer

← drawer

locking slot cut into the side of the drawer

continued ...

UX3 Construction Notes

(A) The floating lock

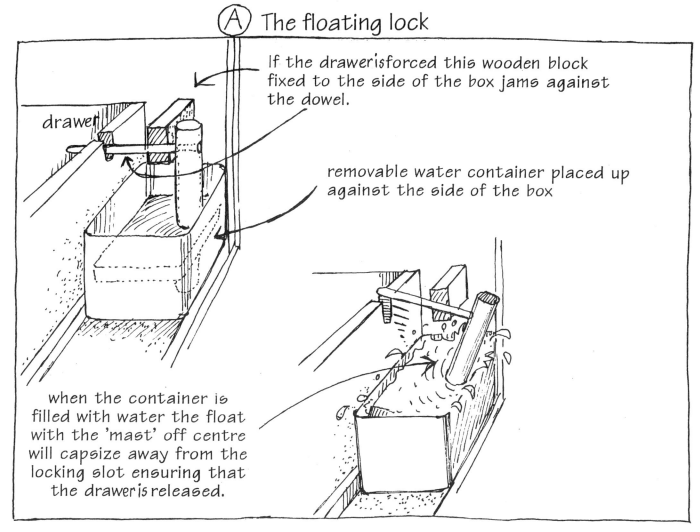

If the drawer is forced this wooden block fixed to the side of the box jams against the dowel.

drawer

removable water container placed up against the side of the box

when the container is filled with water the float with the 'mast' off centre will capsize away from the locking slot ensuring that the drawer is released.

(B) The Bolt Lock

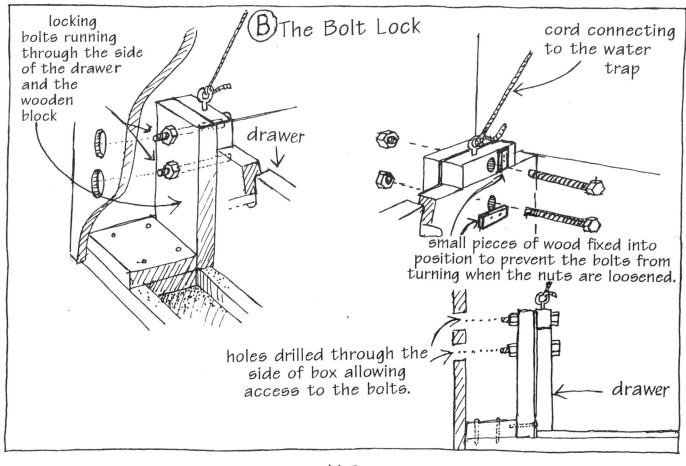

locking bolts running through the side of the drawer and the wooden block

cord connecting to the water trap

drawer

small pieces of wood fixed into position to prevent the bolts from turning when the nuts are loosened.

holes drilled through the side of box allowing access to the bolts.

drawer

UX3 Construction Notes

The balance lock

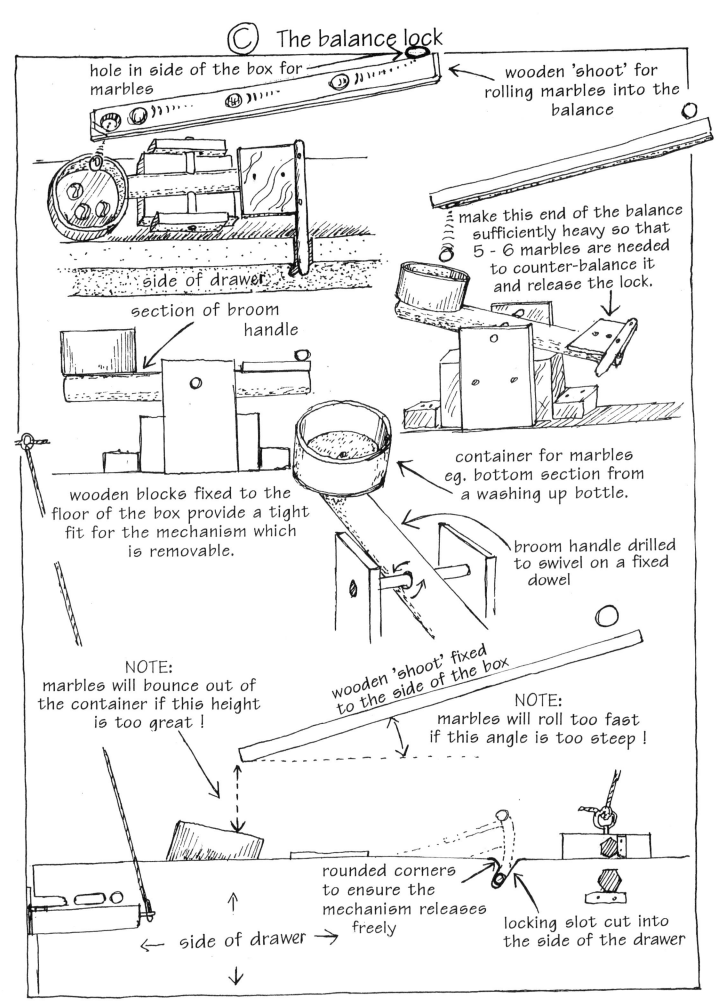

hole in side of the box for marbles

wooden 'shoot' for rolling marbles into the balance

make this end of the balance sufficiently heavy so that 5 - 6 marbles are needed to counter-balance it and release the lock.

side of drawer

section of broom handle

container for marbles eg. bottom section from a washing up bottle.

wooden blocks fixed to the floor of the box provide a tight fit for the mechanism which is removable.

broom handle drilled to swivel on a fixed dowel

NOTE: marbles will bounce out of the container if this height is too great !

wooden 'shoot' fixed to the side of the box

NOTE: marbles will roll too fast if this angle is too steep !

rounded corners to ensure the mechanism releases freely

locking slot cut into the side of the drawer

← side of drawer →

117

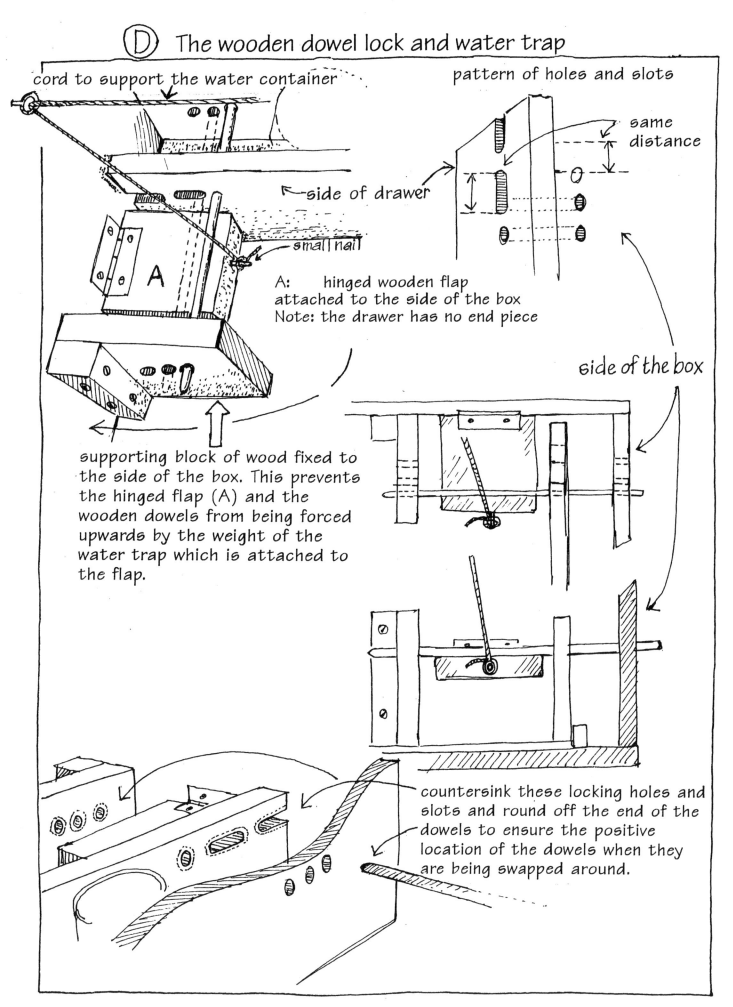

Ⓓ The wooden dowel lock and water trap

cord to support the water container

pattern of holes and slots

same distance

side of drawer

small nail

A: hinged wooden flap
attached to the side of the box
Note: the drawer has no end piece

side of the box

supporting block of wood fixed to
the side of the box. This prevents
the hinged flap (A) and the
wooden dowels from being forced
upwards by the weight of the
water trap which is attached to
the flap.

countersink these locking holes and
slots and round off the end of the
dowels to ensure the positive
location of the dowels when they
are being swapped around.

UX3 Construction Notes

The drawer and water trap

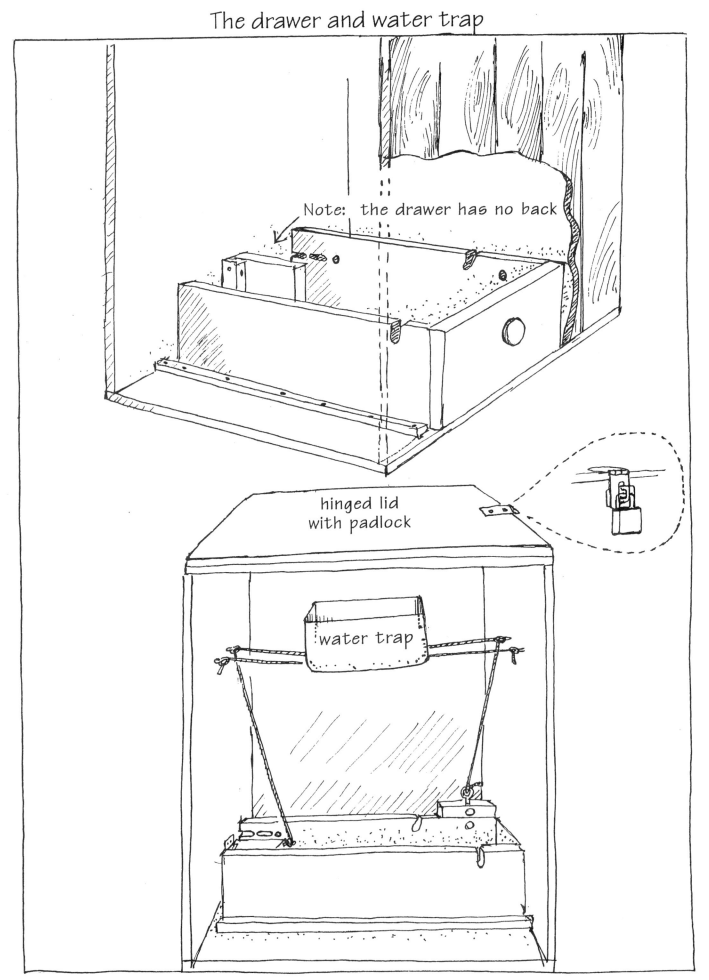

Note: the drawer has no back

hinged lid
with padlock

water trap

The Search for page 50 - The Final Chapter

continued from page 51

continued ...